ELECTRICAL SYSTEMS

DELMAR
CENGAGE Learning™

NATEF Standards Lab Manual - AT 103
Jack Erjavec and Jim Clarke

Vice President, Technology and Trades SBU:
Alar Elken
Editorial Director:
Sandy Clark
Senior Acquisitions Editor:
David Boelio
Developmental Editor:
Christopher Shortt
Director of Marketing:
Dave Garza
Channel Manager:
Bill Lawrensen
Marketing Coordinator:
Mark Pierro
Production Director:
Mary Ellen Black
Production Manager:
Larry Main
Production Coordinator:
Dawn Jacobson
Project Editor:
Toni Hansen
Art-Design Specialist:
Rachel Baker
Editorial Assistant:
Kevin Rivenburg

ISBN-13: 978-1-4018-8113-9

ISBN-10: 1-4018-8113-0

Delmar Cengage Learning
5 Maxwell Drive
Clifton Park, NY 12065-2919
USA

Cengage Learning products are represented in Canada by Nelson Education, Ltd.

For your lifelong learning solutions, visit **delmar.cengage.com**

Visit our corporate website at **www.cengage.com**

Notice to the Reader
Publisher does not warrant or guarantee any of the products described herein or perform any independent analysis in connection with any of the product information contained herein. Publisher does not assume, and expressly disclaims, any obligation to obtain and include information other than that provided to it by the manufacturer. The reader is expressly warned to consider and adopt all safety precautions that might be indicated by the activities described herein and to avoid all potential hazards. By following the instructions contained herein, the reader willingly assumes all risks in connection with such instructions. The publisher makes no representations or warranties of any kind, including but not limited to, the warranties of fitness for particular purpose or merchantability, nor are any such representations implied with respect to the material set forth herein, and the publisher takes no responsibility with respect to such material. The publisher shall not be liable for any special, consequential, or exemplary damages resulting, in whole or part, from the readers' use of, or reliance upon, this material.

Printed in Canada
11 12 13 11 10 09 08

CONTENTS

CHAPTER 19 Charging Systems: Theory, Diagnosis, and Service

CHAPTER 20 Lighting Systems

INTRODUCTION INFORMATION SHEET

AT103 / Electrical Systems

Overview

The electrical systems and components of today's vehicles control virtually every function of the vehicle. It is important that technicians know how to identify the different types of circuits, their control units, and their protection devices.

Basics of Electricity.

Simply put, electricity is the controlled movement of electrons through a conductor. The direction and controlled movement of the electrons is the responsibility of the power source. The number of electrons that are moving in the conductor is determined by the design of the electrical circuit. What the flow of electrons does depends also on the design of the circuit.

To have controlled movement of electrons, there must be a conductor that connects the positive side of the power source to the negative side. There must be a load in the circuit to limit the amount of electron flow.

The natural attraction of electrons to protons is what keeps the electrons moving. The difference between the number of free electrons at the negative side of the power source and the protons at the other side sets up a potential for electron flow or electrical pressure. This pressure is called voltage; the movement of electricity is called current. The load is called the electrical resistance.

Ohm's Law explains the relationship between these three electrical properties (voltage, current, resistance). This law can be used to predict what will happen in a circuit. It can also be used to calculate the value of one of the properties if only two are known. The common expression of Ohm's Law is E (voltage) equals I (current) multiplied by R (resistance), or $E = IR$. An understanding of Ohm's Law is a prerequisite to understanding electricity.

Magnetism

Another electrical term the technician need be familiar with is magnetism. Magnetism is at work in many areas of the vehicle, whether it is in the form of a magnetic field surrounding a permanent magnet or a magnetic field surrounding a conductor which is created by passing an electrical current through a conductor. This is call electromagnetism. In both cases, a magnetic field is present. Permanent magnets are used in components such as wheel speed sensors, analog instrumentation, starters, generators, and vehicle speed sensors. Examples of electromagnetism exhibit themselves in starters, generators, motors, relays, and solenoids. These are examples of magnetism being used in a beneficial way.

Magnetic fields as discussed are present everywhere when current flows through a conductor. There are times when the presence of magnetic lines of force will be a hindrance to a component or system operation. Because an electromagnetic field cuts across several conductors, conductors, that in this case are not part of a specific circuit, unwanted electricity is induced. This phenomenon is called mutual induction, and a majority of times is an unwanted quantity.

When a conductor is formed into a coil, the term "winding" is used. When current is passed through this winding, it will produce a magnetic field around itself; the winding will have a polarity at each end. The polarity of north and south poles will emerge depending on the direction current is flowing through the windings.

The job sheets in this packet acquaint the student with many of the electrical systems procedures covered by the ASE Electrical and Electronics Systems Test. Case studies will encourage and strengthen the student's skill in the use of service manuals and logical diagnostic skills.

INFORMATION SHEET

Ohm's Law

INFORMATION

Ohm's Law is the fundamental law of electricity that is used by the automotive technician to diagnose electrical system problems. A thorough understanding of this important concept is essential to being successful in automotive electrical system repair. This section covers the basic theory and applications to make the student proficient in using Ohm's Law to diagnose common automotive electrical malfunctions.

☐ JOB SHEET / AT 103-1

Using Ohm's Law

Name ______________________ Station ______________ Date ______________

Objective

Upon completion of this job sheet, you will use Ohm's Law to solve circuit problems.

Tools and Materials:

AUTOMOTIVE TECHNOLOGY 4e (Delmar Cengage Learning)

Instructor Notes

Protective Gear:

N/A

NATEF TASKS
VI. Electrical/Electronic Systems
Category: A
Task: 4 (P-1)
Task: 5 (P-1)

PROCEDURE

Using Ohm's Law, solve the following problems:

Problem 1—Series Circuit.

Refer to Figure 1 and solve the problems below.

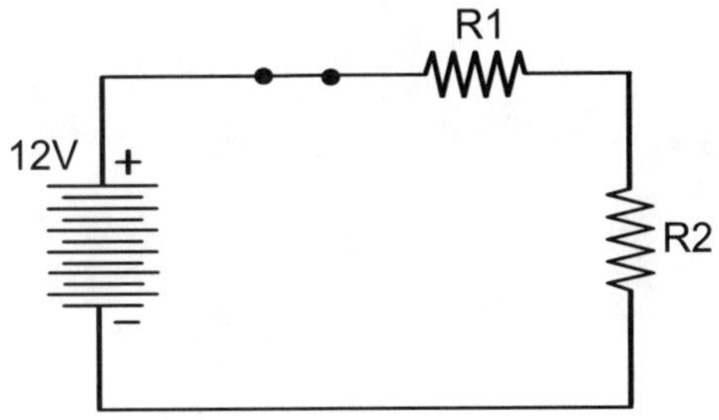

Figure 1. A series circuit.

Calculate the following values, R1 = 2 ohms and R2 = 4 ohms:

Total circuit resistance = ______________________ ohms.

Circuit current = __________________________ amps.

Current through R1 = ______________________ amps.

Current through R2 = ______________________ amps.

Voltage drop across R1 = ___________________ volts.

Voltage drop across R2 = ___________________ volts.

If the resistance of R1 is increased to 8 ohms, what are the new values?

Total circuit resistance = ______________________ ohms.

Circuit current = ____________________________ amps.

Current through R1 = ________________________ amps.

Current through R2 = ________________________ amps.

Voltage drop across R1 = _____________________ volts.

Voltage drop across R2 = ____________________ volts.

Problem 2—Parallel Circuit.

Refer to Figure 2 and solve the problems below.

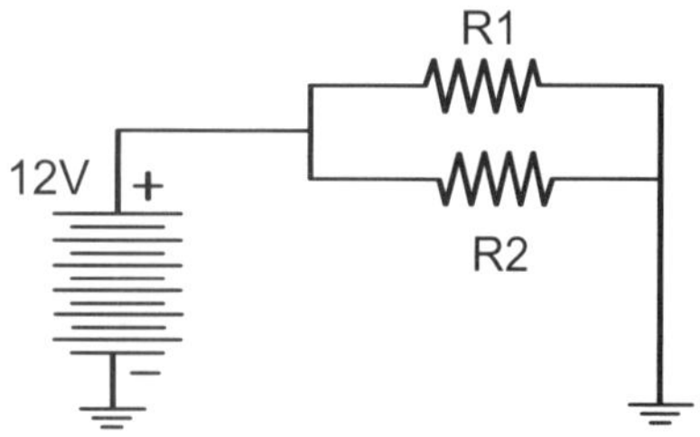

Figure 2. A Parallel Circuit.

Calculate the following values, R1 = 3 ohms and R2 = 6 ohms:

Total circuit resistance = ______________________ ohms.

Circuit current = ____________________________ amps.

Current through R1 = ________________________ amps.

Current through R2 = ________________________ amps.

Voltage drop across R1 = _____________________ volts.

Voltage drop across R2 = ____________________ volts.

Problem 3—Parallel Circuit.

Refer back to Figure 2 and solve the problems below.

Calculate the following values, R1 = 12 ohms and R2 = 12 ohms:

Total circuit resistance = ________________________ ohms.

Circuit current = ______________________________ amps.

Current through R1 = __________________________ amps.

Current through R2 = __________________________ amps.

Voltage drop across R1 = _______________________ volts.

Voltage drop across R2 = ______________________ volts.

Problem 4—Parallel Circuit.

Refer to Figure 3 and solve the problems below.

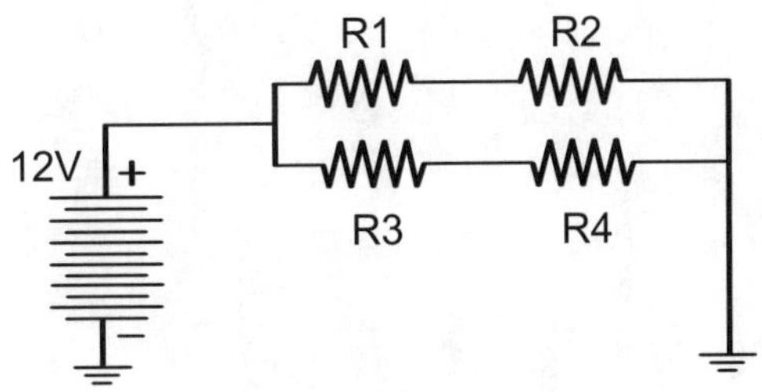

Figure 3. A Parallel Circuit.

Calculate the following values, R1 = 1 ohms, R2 = 3 ohms, R3 = 2 ohms, and R4 = 2 ohms:

Total circuit resistance = ________________________ ohms.

Circuit current = ______________________________ amps.

Current through R1 = __________________________ amps.

Current through R2 = __________________________ amps.

Current through R3 = __________________________ amps.

Current through R4 = __________________________ amps.

Voltage drop across R1 = _______________________ volts.

Voltage drop across R2 = _______________________ volts.

Voltage drop across R3 = _______________________ volts.

Voltage drop across R4 = _______________________ volts.

Problems Encountered

Instructor's Comments

REVIEW QUESTIONS

1. Define the term "electricity."

___

___

___

2. Describe circuit potential.

___

___

___

3. True or False? The current flow is the same throughout a series circuit?

___

4. In a series circuit with a 12-volt power source, a load with a resistance of 6 ohms, and an open ground wire, the circuit current will be ________ amps.

5. True or false? In a parallel circuit, the circuit's current is divided equally between each leg of the parallel circuit.

___

6. True or false? If circuit resistance decreases, circuit current will always increase.

___

7. What is the difference between a mini and maxi fuse circuit application?

___

___

___

8. What is the difference between a permanent magnet and electromagnet?

___

___

___

9. Describe the term "reluctance."

___

___

___

10. Technician A says a higher-than-normal voltage drop is an indication that there is an opening in the circuit. Technician B says excessive and unwanted circuit resistance causes the circuit's current to increase. Who is correct?

    a. Technician A
    b. Technician B
    c. Both A and B
    d. Neither A nor B

INFORMATION SHEET

Batteries: Theory, Diagnosis, Service, and Safety

INFORMATION

Overview

The battery is the heart of a vehicle's electrical system. It supplies current to the starter motor when the engine is being started. It also acts as a voltage stabilizer by supplying current for the lights, radio, and other accessories when the alternator is not handling the load.

In a battery, electrical energy results from a chemical reaction that occurs between two dissimilar plates that are immersed in an electrolyte solution. When a battery is discharging, the battery changes chemical energy into electrical energy. It is through this change that the battery releases stored energy. During charging, electrical energy is converted into chemical energy. As a result, the battery can store the energy as needed.

An automotive battery has three primary functions. It provides voltage and is a source of current for starting, lighting, and ignition. It acts as a voltage stabilizer for the entire electrical system. It also provides current whenever the vehicle's electrical demands exceed the output of the charging system.

The battery must be able to maintain a good charge when the engine is not running. The condition of the battery determines this capacity, as does the electrical demands of the vehicle. When the engine is not running, electrical power is still needed to maintain the memory of the vehicle's computer, clock, stereo, and other electrical devices. The electrical loads present when a vehicle is not running are called parasitic loads. On some vehicles, the parasitic draw is so great that the battery will go dead if the car has not been driven for awhile.

SAFETY PRECAUTIONS

- The acid used in batteries is very toxic and corrosive. Never let the battery acid contact your clothes or skin. Mixing baking soda with the acid can neutralize battery acid. Always have a box of baking soda nearby when working on batteries. If the battery acid contacts your eyes, flush them with water and seek medical attention immediately.
- Always wear safety goggles or glasses when working around batteries (goggles are the preferred eye protection).
- Never place tools on top of the battery, especially on older batteries with the terminals on top. If a tool shorts the terminals, sparks will be produced, and excessive current will heat the tool, possibly causing injury to you or those around you.
- When batteries are discharged and charged, hydrogen gas—which can be highly explosive—develops. Always make a point to keep sparks and flames away from batteries.
- Do not use an excessive charge rate on batteries that are low on electrolytes.
- When disconnecting a battery, always disconnect the negative battery cable first.

- Avoid wearing metal jewelry of any kind when working with batteries; precious metals are some of the best conductors of electricity, and serious injury could result.
- Never attempt to charge a frozen battery. If you suspect the battery of being frozen, place it in a plastic tray and allow the battery to reach room temperature before attempting to charge it. If electrolytes appear in the bottom of your tray, the battery case is cracked, and the battery will have to be replaced.

☐ JOB SHEET / AT 103-2

Inspection of a Battery for Condition, State of Charge, and Capacity

Name ______________________ Station ______________ Date ______________

Objective

Upon completion of this job sheet, you will have demonstrated the ability to inspect and test a battery. You must be able to perform these task(s) in order to pass the **ASE** test for: **Engine Performance and Electrical Systems.** Before beginning to do this Job Sheet, refer to **Chapter 17** in the AUTOMOTIVE TECHNOLOGY book for additional information.

NATEF TASKS
VI. Electrical/Electronic Systems
Category: B
Task: 1 (P-1)
Task: 2 (P-1)

Tools and Materials:

AUTOMOTIVE TECHNOLOGY 4e (Delmar Cengage Learning)
A vehicle with a 12-volt battery
A DMM
Service manual for the above vehicle
Starting/Charging System tester (VAT-40 or similar)

Protective Gear:

Goggles or safety glasses with side shields

Describe the vehicle being worked on:

Year __________ Make ____________________ Model ____________________

VIN ____________________ Engine type and size ____________________

PROCEDURE

1. Describe the general appearance of the battery.

____

____

____

____

2. Describe the general appearance of the cables and terminals.

____

____

____

____

3. Check the tightness of the cables, at both ends. Describe their condition.

____

____

4. Connect the positive lead of the meter (set on DC volts) to the positive terminal of the battery. ☐ Task completed

5. Put the negative lead on the battery case and move it all around the top and sides of the case. What readings do you get on the voltmeter?

____

____

6. What is indicated by the readings?

____

____

7. Measure the voltage of the battery. Your reading was: ___________ volts

8. What do you know about the condition and the state of charge of the battery based on the visual inspection and the above tests?

____

____

____

____

9. Connect the Starting/Charging System tester to the battery. ☐ Task completed

10. Locate the CCA rating of the battery. What is the rating? ___________

11. Based on the CCA, how much load should be put on the battery during the capacity test? _______________ amps

12. Conduct battery load test. ☐ Task completed

    Battery voltage decreased to _______ volts after ________ seconds.

13. Describe the results of the battery load (capacity) test. Include in the results your service recommendations and the reasons for them.

____

____

____

____

Problems Encountered

____

____

____

Instructor's Comments

____

____

____

☐ JOB SHEET / AT 103-3

Charge a Maintenance-Free Battery

Name ______________________ Station ______________ Date ______________

Objective

Upon completion of this job sheet, you will demonstrate the ability to charge a maintenance-free battery. You must be able to perform these task(s) in order to pass the **ASE** test for: **Engine Performance and Electrical Systems.** Before beginning to do this Job Sheet, refer to **Chapter 17** in the AUTOMOTIVE TECHNOLOGY book for additional information.

NATEF TASKS
VI. Electrical/Electronic Systems
Category: B
Task: 5 (P-2)

Tools and Materials:

AUTOMOTIVE TECHNOLOGY 4e (Delmar Cengage Learning)
Baking soda
Battery charger and cables and adapters for side terminal batteries
Battery clamp puller
Battery cleaning wire brush
Battery strap or carrier
Box wrench (1/2-in.) (13 mm) or cable-clamp pliers
Conventional wire brush and rags
Fender covers
Masking tape or bright felt marker
Service manual
Voltmeter

Protective Gear:

Gloves
Rubber apron
Safety goggles, face shield, or safety glasses with side shields

PROCEDURE

CAUTION: *Special care must be given to charging maintenance-free batteries. If any electrolyte is lost during the charging process, the life of the battery is shortened. The fast-rate charge for this type of battery should be limited to 35 amperes for 20 minutes.*

1. Place fender covers around the work area. Remove battery from vehicle as described in Job Sheet 13–1. It is also possible to charge a battery in the vehicle. If performing an in-vehicle charge, consult the service manual for any precautions associated with computer controls. ☐ Task completed

2. Check that the charger is turned off. Connect the positive (+) cable from the charger to the positive (+) battery terminal. Connect the (–) cable from the charger to the negative (–) battery terminal. Be sure you have a good connection to prevent sparking. ☐ Task completed

3. If at no-load the battery reads below 12.2 volts, charge the battery according to the following rates: ☐ Task completed

Battery Capacity (Reserve Minutes)	Slow Charge
80 minutes or less	10 hours at 5 amperes, or 5 hours at 10 amperes
Above 80–125 minutes	15 hours at 5 amperes, or 7-1/2 hours at 10 amperes
Above 125–170 minutes	20 hours at 5 amperes, or 10 hours at 10 amperes
Above 170–250 minutes	30 hours at 5 amperes, or 15 hours at 10 amperes
Above 250 minutes	20 hours at 10 amperes

If the voltage of the battery at room temperature is 12.2 volts, charge the battery for half the time shown under "Slow Charge." If the voltage is 12.4 volts, charge the battery for one-fourth the "Slow Charge" time.

Turn the clock control on the charger to the desired charging time. Do not exceed the manufacturer's battery-charging limits, which generally appear on battery.

4. Charge the battery to a voltage of at least 12.6 volts or until the green ball appears. Shaking or tipping the battery may be necessary to make the green ball appear. Never overcharge a battery. ☐ Task completed

   WARNING: *Never smoke around a charging battery. The hydrogen gas produced is highly explosive.*

5. When the battery is fully charged, turn off the power switch and disconnect the two battery charger cables from the battery. Return the charger to the proper area. ☐ Task completed

Problems Encountered

____

____

____

Instructor's Comments

____

____

____

☐ JOB SHEET / AT 103-4

Remove, Clean, and Replace a Battery

Name ______________________ Station ______________ Date ______________

Objective

Upon completion of this job sheet, you will demonstrate the ability to properly and safely remove, clean, and replace a battery. You must be able to perform these task(s) in order to pass the **ASE** test for: **Engine Performance and Electrical Systems.** Before beginning to do this Job Sheet, refer to **Chapter 17** in the AUTOMOTIVE TECHNOLOGY book for additional information.

Tools and Materials:

AUTOMOTIVE TECHNOLOGY 4e (Delmar Cengage Learning)

Baking soda

Battery clamp puller

Battery cleaning wire brush

Battery strap or carrier

Box wrench (1/2-in.) (13 mm) or cable-clamp pliers

Conventional wire brush and rags

Fender covers

Masking tape or bright felt marker

Corrosion Protective Spray

Service manual

NATEF TASKS
VI. Electrical/Electronic Systems
Category: B
Task: 6 (P-1)

Protective Gear:

Rubber gloves

Rubber apron

Face shield, goggles, or safety glasses with side shields

Describe the vehicle being worked on:

Year ________ Make ____________________ Model ____________________

VIN ____________________ Engine type and size ____________________

PROCEDURE

1. Place a fender cover around the work area. ☐ Task completed

2. Consult the appropriate service manual for precautions about computer controls. ☐ Task completed

3. Remove the negative (–) battery terminal. For connectors tightened with nuts and bolts, loosen the nut with a box wrench or cable-clamp pliers (Figure 4A). Using ordinary pliers or an open-end wrench can cause problems. Always grip the cable while loosening the nut. This will prevent unnecessary pressure on the terminal post that could break it or loosen its mounting in the battery. If the connector does not lift easily off the terminal when loosened, use a clamp puller to free it (Figure 4B). Prying with a screwdriver or bar strains the terminal post. ☐ Task completed

Figure 4. Removing a battery.

4. Loosen the positive (+) battery cable and remove it from the battery with a battery terminal puller. If both battery cables are the same color, it is wise to mark the positive cable so that you will connect it to the correct terminal later. All that is needed to mark the cable is masking or similar kind of tape. Although differences in terminal size are designed to prevent reversing the polarity of the battery, marking the positive cable is an extra safeguard. ☐ Task completed

5. Loosen and remove the battery holddown straps, cover, and heat shield (Figure 4C). ☐ Task completed

6. Lift the battery from the battery tray using a battery strap or carrier (Figure 4D). ☐ Task completed

7. Clean and inspect the battery tray using a solution of baking soda and water. ☐ Task completed

8. Clean the battery cable terminals with baking soda solution and a battery terminal brush. Use the external portion to clean the post (Figure 5A) and internal portion for the terminal ends (Figure 5B). ☐ Task completed

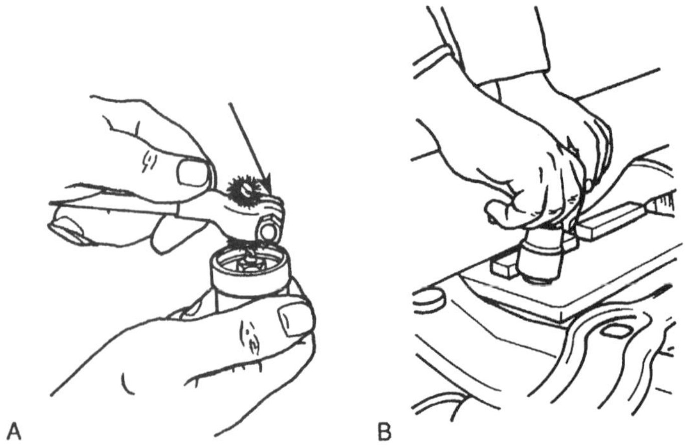

Figure 5. Cleaning battery cable terminals with baking soda solution and a battery terminal brush.

☐ JOB SHEET / AT 103-5

Jump-Starting a Vehicle

Name ______________________ Station ______________ Date ______________

Objective

Upon completion of this job sheet, you will be able to start a vehicle using jumper cables and another vehicle. You must be able to perform these task(s) in order to pass the **ASE** test for: **Electrical and Electronic Systems.** Before beginning to do this Job Sheet, refer to **Chapter 17** in the AUTOMOTIVE TECHNOLOGY book for additional information.

NATEF TASKS
VI. Electrical/Electronic Systems
Category: B
Task: 7 (P-1)

Tools and Materials:

AUTOMOTIVE TECHNOLOGY 4e (Delmar Cengage Learning)

Jumper cables

Protective Gear:

Goggles or safety glasses with side shields

Describe the vehicle being worked on:

Year __________ Make ____________________ Model ____________________

VIN ____________________ Engine type and size ____________________

PROCEDURE

1. Make sure the two vehicles are not touching each other. ☐ Task completed
2. Apply the parking brake for each vehicle and put the transmissions in neutral or park. ☐ Task completed
3. Turn off the ignition switch and the accessories on both vehicles. ☐ Task completed
4. Attach one end of the positive jumper cable to the disabled battery's positive terminal. ☐ Task completed
5. Connect the other end of the positive jumper cable to the booster battery's positive terminal. ☐ Task completed
6. Attach one end of the negative jumper cable to the booster battery's negative terminal. ☐ Task completed
7. Attach the other end of the negative jumper cable to an engine ground on the disabled vehicle. ☐ Task completed
8. Attempt to start the disabled vehicle. If the disabled vehicle does not readily start, start the jumper vehicle and run it at fast idle. ☐ Task completed
9. Once the disabled vehicle starts, disconnect the ground connected negative jumper cable from the engine block. ☐ Task completed
10. Disconnect the negative jumper cable from the booster battery. ☐ Task completed
11. Disconnect the positive jumper cable from the booster battery, then from the other battery. ☐ Task completed

Problems Encountered

Instructor's Comments

CASE STUDY

The customer complains that his battery is "dead" every morning. What could be the problem and what can be done to find the cause of the problem?

REVIEW QUESTIONS

1. What is a parasitic load?

____

____

2. What are you measuring when you measure open-circuit battery voltage?

____

____

3. Technician A says a corroded battery terminal connector can prevent the battery from supplying enough voltage for the vehicle. Technician B says dirt on a battery can cause the battery to drain. Who is correct?

   a. Technician A
   b. Technician B
   c. Both A and B
   d. Neither A nor B

4. True or false? When time is available, slow-charging is preferable to fast charging. ____________

5. True or false? Battery capacity or efficiency is improved by cold weather.

____

6. Batteries can ____________________ when exposed to sparks and open flames when charging.

7. The ____________________ cable is always removed first.

8. The best cleaning solution for cleaning a battery is ________________.

9. The ________________________ test is a more accurate indication of battery condition than either the specific gravity or open-voltage test.

10. What does a battery capacity test measure?

____

____

INFORMATION SHEET

Electrical Systems Diagnostics and Service

INFORMATION

Overview

Diagnosing electrical and electronics in automotive systems requires a broad base of skills, knowledge, and understanding. The skills required for such system diagnosis include reading and comprehending service manual electrical schematics, knowing how to operate a variety of test equipment, understanding the benefits of using a logical, systematic approach to troubleshooting system faults, and testing system components in order to determine and correct the system fault.

Electrical Problems

Electrical problems (concerns) of the automobile will focus in one of three areas: opens, shorts, and high resistance. The "open" being a broken wire or disconnected terminal; the "short" being a short to power or a short to ground; and "high resistance" is a corroded frayed, or loose connection. Each of these area faults will limit or eliminate the operation of the circuit.

An open is a problem caused by an incomplete circuit. With an open there is no current flow because the circuit is not connected to both sides of the power source or battery. Because there is no current flow, the load in the circuit does not operate.

Switches are used to open and close circuits. All a switch does is complete or open the circuit. When a wire becomes disconnected or broken, the circuit will be open and current will not flow. A good example of this is a burned-out bulb. When a bulb is burned out, the filament, which is a special conductor, is open. An open is normally indicated by the fact that something is not working.

Another possible electrical problem is excessively high resistance. This results from poor connections, frayed wires, or corrosion at a connection. With the added resistance, circuit current is lowered and the load (appliance) in the circuit cannot operate normally. High resistance problems are normally indicated by reduced operation, such as a dim headlight.

The third possible problem is a short. A short is an unwanted path to ground. This path can be caused by a wire making direct contact with ground or can be caused by a wire making contact with another wire in the circuit. As a result of this additional path, circuit resistance is decreased and circuit current increases. Typically, this increase will cause the circuit protection device (fuse, circuit breaker, or fusible link) to open.

Electrical Diagrams

Electrical diagrams or schematics are system maps that indicate the power side of the circuit, switch(es), the component(s), and the groundside of the circuit. Color-coded wiring connects the battery source through the switch to the component through to the ground. Electrical schematics are used in conjunction with troubleshooting charts to pinpoint and repair the electrical system fault.

Electrical Testing Tools

A technician is required to operate a variety of electrical test equipment to determine the problem in a specific electrical circuit. The tools include circuit testers, voltmeters, ammeters, ohmmeters, and other test equipment such as jumper wires, variable resistors, volt/ampere testers, scan tools, computer memory savers, multimeters, and lab scopes.

Testing Basic Electrical Components

The basic electrical components include the testing of protection devices such as fuses, circuit breakers, thermisters, switches, relays and stepped resistors, variable resistors, wiring, and printed circuits.

Troubleshooting Circuits

The troubleshooting of an electrical circuit begins with the verification of the customer's concern. If it is found that the electrical system is not operating properly, then the process to find and repair the fault begins. When following a troubleshooting chart for the identified electrical system, the chart may require testing for an open, short, or high resistance depending on your findings during the testing procedure.

Protecting Electronic Systems

When handling and testing electronic components, it is possible to inadvertently damage the component due to voltage surges or spikes. Electrostatic discharge is one way of creating damage to the electronic component. The use of static discharge straps and mats will greatly reduce this possibility. Voltage surge is possible if an electronic device is disconnected from a circuit while power is flowing through the circuit. Ensure the ignition is off or that the power source is disabled before disconnecting or reconnecting electronic components.

Testing Electronic Systems and Circuits

Multimeters and lab scopes are two of the most common pieces of test equipment used for testing electronic circuits and systems. A majority of the electronic circuit testing would involve the use of the multimeter. The various functions of the meter allow for testing of such things as diodes, frequency, and RMS (root-means-square) for AC circuits for voltage and amperage reading. The lab scope is used to aid in the diagnosis of fuel pump and fuel injector patterns.

Connector and Wire Repair

Many of the vehicle's electrical faults can be traced to faulty wiring and connectors. When the vehicle is new, the wiring and connector problems may be loose connections caused by connectors not properly seated, wire terminals in the connector not properly seated or loose grounds. As the vehicle ages, frayed wires and corrosion are more common faults with the wiring and connectors. Correction of these faults may require the replacement of the terminal end by crimping and/or soldering. In testing electrical systems the wiring circuits to and from the electronic component are tested first because the wiring circuitry may be the cause of the damaged electronic component.

☐ JOB SHEET / AT 103-6

Check Continuity in a Circuit with a Test Light

Name ______________________ Station ______________ Date ______________

OBJECTIVE

Upon completion of this job sheet, you will have demonstrated the ability to test continuity in a circuit with a test light. You must be able to perform these task(s) in order to pass the **ASE** test for: **Electrical Systems.** Before beginning to do this Job Sheet, refer to **Chapter 16** in the AUTOMOTIVE TECHNOLOGY book for additional information.

WARNING: *Never use a regular test light on an electronic circuit; use only a high-impedance test light on these circuits.*

Tools and Materials:

AUTOMOTIVE TECHNOLOGY 4e (Delmar Cengage Learning)

Test light

Wiring diagram

Service manual

NATEF TASKS
VI. Electrical/Electronic Systems
Category: A
Task: 3 (P-1)
Task: 7 (P-2)

Protective Gear:

Goggles or safety glasses with side shields

Describe the vehicle being worked on:

Year ________ Make __________________ Model __________________

VIN __________________ Engine type and size __________________

PROCEDURE

1. Determine if the circuit to be tested is a power supply circuit or a ground circuit. ☐ Task completed
2. If the circuit to be tested is a power supply circuit, connect the clip end of the test light to a ground on the vehicle. ☐ Task completed
3. Turn the key to the on position. ☐ Task completed
4. With the light end, use the probe to check the wire in the circuit at each connector in the specific circuit. ☐ Task completed
5. If the test light comes on, there is continuity between the power supply and the point where you are testing. ☐ Task completed
6. If the circuit to be tested is a ground circuit, connect the clip end of the test light to a power supply, such as the battery. ☐ Task completed
7. With the light end, use the probe to check the wire in the circuit at each connector in the specific circuit. ☐ Task completed

8. If the test light comes on, there is continuity between the ground and the point you are testing. ☐ Task completed

Problems Encountered

____

____

____

Instructor's Comments

____

____

____

☐ JOB SHEET / AT 103-7

Testing for Voltage with a DMM

Name ______________________ Station ______________ Date ______________

Objective

Upon completion of this job sheet, you will be able to measure available voltage and voltage drop with a DMM. You must be able to perform these task(s) in order to pass the **ASE** test for: **Electrical Systems.** Before beginning to do this Job Sheet, refer to **Chapter 16** in the AUTOMOTIVE TECHNOLOGY book for additional information.

WARNING: *Use only a high-impedance DMM on late-model vehicles.*

NATEF TASKS
VI. Electrical/Electronic Systems
Category: A
Task: 8 (P-1)

Tools and Materials:

AUTOMOTIVE TECHNOLOGY 4e (Delmar Cengage Learning)
DMM
Wiring diagram for vehicle
Basic hand tools

Protective Gear:

Goggles or safety glasses with side shields

Describe the vehicle being worked on:

Year ________ Make ____________________ Model ____________________

VIN ____________________ Engine type and size ____________________

PROCEDURE

1. Set the DMM to the appropriate scale to read 12 volts DC. ☐ Task completed
2. Connect the meter across the battery (positive to positive and negative to negative)

   What is your reading on the meter? __________ volts
3. With the meter still connected across the battery, turn on the headlights of the vehicle.

   What is your reading on the meter? __________ volts
4. Keep the headlights on.

   Connect the positive lead of the meter to the point on the vehicle where the battery's ground cable attaches to the frame. Keep the negative lead where it is.

   What is your reading on the meter? __________ volts

   What is being measured? ______________________________

5. Disconnect the meter from the battery and turn off the headlights. ☐ Task completed

6. Refer to the correct wiring diagram and determine what wire at the right headlight delivers current to the lamp when the headlights are on and low beams selected.

   Color of the wire ______________________________

7. From the wiring diagram identify where the headlight is grounded.

   Place of ground ______________________________

8. Connect the negative lead of the meter to the point where the headlight is grounded. ☐ Task completed

9. Connect the positive lead of the meter to the power input of the headlight. ☐ Task completed

10. Turn on the headlights.

    What is your reading on the meter? __________ volts

    What is being measured? ______________________________

11. What is the difference between the reading here and the battery's voltage?

    __________ volts

12. Explain why there is a difference.

    ____

    ____

    ____

    ____

Problems Encountered

____

____

____

Instructor's Comments

____

____

____

☐ JOB SHEET / AT 103-8

Testing Voltage Drop Across Connectors

Name ______________________ Station ______________ Date ______________

Objective

Upon completion of this job sheet, you will demonstrate the ability to check voltage drop across a connector. You must be able to perform these task(s) in order to pass the **ASE** test for: **Electrical Systems.**

NATEF TASKS
VI. Electrical/Electronic Systems
Category: A
Task: 8 (P-1)

Tools and Materials:

AUTOMOTIVE TECHNOLOGY 4e (Delmar Cengage Learning)
DMM
Wiring diagrams
Service manual

Protective Gear:

Goggles or safety glasses with side shields

Describe the vehicle being worked on:

Year ________ Make ________________ Model ________________

VIN ________________ Engine type and size ________________

PROCEDURE

1. Determine the connector to be tested. ☐ Task completed
2. Turn on the ignition to supply power to the circuit. ☐ Task completed
3. Set the DMM on the proper voltage scale. ☐ Task completed
4. Connect the negative lead (the black lead) of the meter to a ground on the vehicle. ☐ Task completed
5. Use the positive lead (the red lead) to check the voltage at one side of the connector. ☐ Task completed
6. Record the voltage. ☐ Task completed
7. Use the positive lead (the red lead) to check the voltage at the other side of the connector. ☐ Task completed
8. Record the voltage. ☐ Task completed
9. If there is a difference subtract the lower voltage from the higher voltage. ☐ Task completed
10. Compare this difference with the specifications in the service manual to determine if the difference is within specifications. ☐ Task completed

Problems Encountered

Instructor's Comments

☐ JOB SHEET / AT 103-9

Inspect and Test Fuses, Fusible Links, and Circuit Breakers

Name ______________________ Station ______________ Date ______________

Objective

Upon completion of this job sheet, you will have the ability to inspect and check fuses, fusible links, and circuit breakers. You must be able to perform these task(s) in order to pass the **ASE** test for: **Electrical Systems.**

NATEF TASKS
VI. Electrical/Electronic Systems
Category: A
Task: 14 (P-1)

Tools and Materials:

AUTOMOTIVE TECHNOLOGY 4e (Delmar Cengage Learning)

DMM

Test light

Service manual

Protective Gear:

Goggles or safety glasses with side shields

Describe the vehicle being worked on:

Year __________ Make ______________________ Model ______________________

VIN ______________________ Engine type and size ______________________

PROCEDURE

1. Visually check fuses. ☐ Task completed
2. Using a test light to test a fuse, ground the clip on one end of the test light. Touch the probe to each end of the fuse. If the light comes on at both ends of the fuse, it is good. If the light only works when touched to one end of the fuse, it is bad. Replace it. ☐ Task completed
3. Using a test light to test a fusible link, ground the clip on one end of the test light. Touch the probe to each end of the fusible link. If the light comes on at both ends of the fusible link, it is good. If the light only comes on at one end of the fusible link, it is bad. Replace it. ☐ Task completed
4. Using a DMM to test a fuse or fusible link can be done two different ways. ☐ Task completed
5. If you are using the voltage scale, you will connect the black lead (the negative lead) to a ground. ☐ Task completed
6. Touch the red lead, positive lead, to each end of the fuse or fusible link. ☐ Task completed
7. If the voltage reading is the same at both ends, the fuse or fusible link is good. ☐ Task completed

8. If you only get a voltage reading at one end, the fuse or fusible link is bad. Replace it. ☐ Task completed

9. If you are using the ohmmeter to test a fuse or circuit breaker, the procedure is different. ☐ Task completed

10. Remove the fuse or circuit breaker. ☐ Task completed

11. Touch the leads from the meter to each end of the fuse or circuit breaker. ☐ Task completed

12. If there is continuity, the fuse or circuit breaker is good. ☐ Task completed

13. If there is no continuity, the fuse or circuit breaker is bad. Replace it. ☐ Task completed

Problems Encountered

___

___

___

Instructor's Comments

___

___

___

☐ JOB SHEET / AT 103-10

Part Identification on a Wiring Diagram

Name ______________________ Station ______________ Date ______________

Objective

Upon completion of this job sheet, you will be able to locate different parts on a wiring diagram. You must be able to perform these task(s) in order to pass the **ASE** test for: **Electrical Systems.** Before beginning to do this Job Sheet, refer to **Chapter 14** in the AUTOMOTIVE TECHNOLOGY book for additional information.

NATEF TASKS
VI. Electrical/Electronic Systems
Category: A
Task: 5 (P-1)

Tools and Materials:

AUTOMOTIVE TECHNOLOGY 4e (Delmar Cengage Learning)

A wiring diagram in a service manual (assigned by the instructor)

Protection Gear:

N/A

Type of Vehicle:

Year ________ Make ____________________ Model ____________________

Service manual used: ____________________

Wiring diagram is found on pages: ________ to ________ .

PROCEDURE

Look over the wiring diagram, then answer the following questions:

1. Are all circuit grounds clearly marked in the wiring diagrams? ____________________
2. What is represented by lines that cross other lines?
   ____
   ____
3. Are most switches shown in their normally open or normally closed position?
   ____
4. Do all wires have a color code listed by them? ____________________
5. Is the internal circuitry of all components shown in their schematical drawing? __________

List the page and figure numbers (the location) where the following electrical components are shown in the wiring diagram. Then **draw the schematical symbol** used by this wiring diagram to represent the part.

Component	Location	Drawing
Windshield wiper motor	____________	____________
Dome (courtesy) light	____________	____________
A/C compressor clutch	____________	____________
Turn signal flasher unit	____________	____________
Fuse	____________	____________
Fuel gauge sending unit	____________	____________

Problems Encountered

Instructor's Comments

☐ JOB SHEET / AT 103-11

Soldering Two Copper Wires Together

Name ______________________ Station ______________ Date ______________

Objective

Upon completion of this job sheet, you will be able to make wire repairs using solder. You must be able to perform these task(s) in order to pass the **ASE** test for: **Electrical Systems.** Before beginning to do this Job Sheet, refer to **Chapter 14** in the AUTOMOTIVE TECHNOLOGY book for additional information.

Tools and Materials:

AUTOMOTIVE TECHNOLOGY 4e (Delmar Cengage Learning)

100-watt soldering iron

60/40 Rosin core solder

Crimping tool

Splice clip

Heat shrink tube

Heating gun

NATEF TASKS
VI. Electrical/Electronic Systems
Category: A
Task: 16 (P-1)
Task: 17 (P-1)

Protective Gear:

Goggles or safety glasses with side shields

PROCEDURE

1. Disconnect the fuse that powers the circuit being repaired. **NOTE:** *If a fuse does not protect the circuit, disconnect the ground lead of the battery.* What did you need to do?

   ____

   ____

2. Locate and cut out the damaged wire. Where is the wire and what circuit does it belong to?

   ____

   ____

3. Using the correct size stripper, remove about 1/2-inch of the insulation from both wires. ☐ Task completed

4. Now remove about 1/2-inch of the insulation from both ends of the replacement wire. The length of the replacement wire should be slightly longer than the length of the wire removed. What size wire are you inserting to make the repair?

   ____

   ____

5. Select the proper size splice clip to hold the splice. ☐ Task completed

6. Place the correct size and length of heat shrink tube over the two ends of the wire. ☐ Task completed
7. Overlap the two spliced ends and center the splice clip around the wires, making sure the wires extend beyond the splice clip in both directions. ☐ Task completed
8. Crimp the splice clip firmly in place. ☐ Task completed
9. Heat the splice clip with the soldering iron while applying solder to the opening of the clip. Do not apply solder to the iron. The iron should be 180 degrees away from the opening of the clip. ☐ Task completed
10. After the solder cools, check the integrity of the joint. How did you do that?

    ____

    ____

11. Slide the heat shrink tube over the splice. ☐ Task completed
12. Heat the tube with the hot air gun until it shrinks around the splice. Do not overheat the heat shrink tube. Describe any problems you faced:

    ____

    ____

    ____

Problems Encountered

____

____

____

Instructor's Comments

____

____

____

☐ JOB SHEET / AT 103-12

Connector and Wire Repairs

Name ______________________ Station ______________ Date ______________

Objective

Upon completion of this job sheet, you will be able to repair wiring harnesses and connectors. You must be able to perform these task(s) in order to pass the **ASE** test for: **Electrical and Electronic Systems.** Before beginning to do this Job Sheet, refer to **Chapter 14** in the AUTOMOTIVE TECHNOLOGY book for additional information.

Tools and Materials:

AUTOMOTIVE TECHNOLOGY 4e (Delmar Cengage Learning)

Crimping tool

Dielectric grease

Heat shrink tubing

Electrical tape

NATEF TASKS

VI. Electrical/Electronic Systems

Category: A

Task: 16 (P-1)

Task 17: (P-1)

Protective Gear:

Goggles or safety glasses with side shields

Describe the vehicle being worked on:

Year ________ Make ____________________ Model ____________________

VIN ____________________ Engine type and size ____________________

PROCEDURE

NOTE: *The preferred way to connect wires or to install a connector is by soldering.*

1. Check all connectors for corrosion, dirt, and looseness. Describe your findings.

____

____

2. Nearly all connectors have pushdown release type locks. Make sure these are not damaged when disconnecting the connectors. Refer to the service manual for the correct way to open and release a wire from the connectors on the vehicle. Summarize that procedure.

____

____

3. Check the wiring for loose or corroded terminals; frayed, broken, or oil-soaked wires; and faulty insulation. Describe your findings.

____

____

WARNING: *Always follow the vehicle manufacturer's wiring and terminal repair procedure given in the service manual. On some components and circuits, manufacturers recommend component* *replacement rather than wiring repairs.*

4. To replace a connector or to repair a wire by using a connector, begin by selecting the appropriate size and type of terminal connector. Be sure it is suitable for the unit's connecting post or prongs and it has enough current-carrying capacity for the circuit. Also, make sure it is heavy enough to endure normal wire flexing and vibration. ☐ Task completed

5. Use the correct stripping opening on the crimping tool for the gauge of the wire and remove enough wire insulation to allow the wire to completely penetrate the connector. ☐ Task completed

6. Place the wire into the connector and crimp the connector. To get a proper crimp, place the open area of the connector facing toward the anvil. Make sure the wire is compressed under the crimp. ☐ Task completed

7. Insert the stripped end of the other wire into the connector, if connecting two wires, and crimp in the same manner. ☐ Task completed

8. Use electrical tape or heat shrink tubing to tightly seal the connection. This will provide good protection for the wire and connector. ☐ Task completed

9. When working with wiring and connectors, never pull on the wires to separate the connectors. This can create an intermittent contact and an intermittent problem that may be very difficult to find later. When required, always use the special tools designed for separating connectors. ☐ Task completed

10. Never reroute wires when making repairs. Rerouting wires can result in induced voltages in nearby components. These stray voltages can interfere with the functioning of electronic circuits. ☐ Task completed

11. Apply dielectric grease to moisture proof and to protect connections from corrosion. Some car manufacturers suggest using petroleum jelly to protect connection points. ☐ Task completed

Problems Encountered

____

____

____

Instructor's Comments

____

____

____

☐ JOB SHEET / AT 103-13

Test for Continuity Across Electronic and Electrical Components and Circuits with an Ohmmeter

Name ____________________ Station ______________ Date ______________

Objective

Upon completion of this job sheet, you will have demonstrated the ability to check continuity on electronic and electrical components with an ohmmeter. You must be able to perform these task(s) in order to pass the **ASE** test for: **Electrical Systems and Engine Performance.** Before beginning to do this Job Sheet, refer to **Chapter 15** in the AUTOMOTIVE TECHNOLOGY book for additional information.

NATEF TASKS
VI. Electrical/Electronic Systems
Category: A
Task: 10 (P-1)

Tools and Materials:

AUTOMOTIVE TECHNOLOGY 4e (Delmar Cengage Learning)

A vehicle

A DMM

An analog ohmmeter

Wiring diagram for the vehicle

NOTE: *An ohmmeter works by sending a small amount of current through the path to be measured. Because of this, all circuits and components being tested must be disconnected from power. An ohmmeter must never be connected to an energized circuit; doing so may damage the meter. The safest way to measure ohms is to disconnect the negative battery cable before taking resistance readings.*

Protective Gear:

Goggles or safety glasses with side shields

Describe the vehicle being worked on:

Year ________ Make ________________ Model ________________

VIN ________________ Engine type and size ________________

PROCEDURE

1. Locate the fuse panel or power distribution box. ☐ Task completed
2. With no power to the fuses, check the resistance of each fuse. Summarize your findings:

   ____

   ____

   ____

3. Now connect the leads of the analog meter across the negative battery cable.

   Your reading is: _______ ohms

Now connect the leads of the digital meter across the negative battery cable.

Your reading is: ________ ohms

4. Disconnect the wires leading to the ignition coil.

   Now connect the leads of the analog meter across the terminals of the coil.

   Your reading is: ________ ohms

   Now connect the leads of the digital meter across the terminals of the coil.

   Your reading is: ________ ohms

5. Reconnect the wires to the coil.

   Carefully remove one spark plug wire from the spark plug and the ignition coil or distributor cap.

   Now connect the leads of the analog meter across the wire.

   Your reading is: ________ ohms

   Now connect the leads of the digital meter across the wire.

   Your reading is: ________ ohms

6. Carefully reinstall the spark plug wire.

   Locate the cigar lighter inside the vehicle.

   Now connect the leads of the analog meter from the heating coil to its case.

   Your reading is: ________ ohms

   Now connect the leads of the digital meter from the heating coil to its case.

   Your reading is: ________ ohms

7. Refer to the service manual and find out how to remove the bulb in the dome light.

   Remove it.

   Now connect the leads of the analog meter across the bulb.

   Your reading is: ________ ohms

   Now connect the leads of the digital meter across the bulb.

   Your reading is: ________ ohms

8. Reinstall the bulb.

   Remove the rear brake light bulb.

   Now connect the leads of the analog meter across the bulb.

   Your reading is: ________ ohms

   Now connect the leads of the digital meter across the bulb.

   Your reading is: ________ ohms

9. Reinstall the bulb

   Disconnect the wire connector to one of the headlights.

From the wiring diagram, identify which terminals are for low beam operation.

Now connect the leads of the analog meter across the low beam terminals.

Your reading is: ________ ohms

Now connect the leads of the digital meter across the low beam terminals.

Your reading is: ________ ohms

10. From the wiring diagram, identify which terminals are for high beam operation.

    Now connect the leads of the analog meter across the high beam terminals.

    Your reading is: ________ ohms

    Now connect the leads of the digital meter across the high beam terminals.

    Your reading is: ________ ohms

11. You should have gotten slightly different readings from the digital meter and the analog meter. Explain why.

    ____

    ____

    ____

    ____

12. You measured the resistance across several different light bulbs. On each you should have read a different amount of resistance. Based on your findings, which light bulb would be the brightest and which would be the dimmest. Explain why.

    ____

    ____

    ____

    ____

    ____

    ____

Problems Encountered

____

____

____

Instructor's Comments

____

____

____

REVIEW QUESTIONS

1. True or false? A test light can be used to check all circuits on today's vehicles. ________________

2. What is the difference between voltage and current?

____

____

3. Technician A says higher than normal voltage drops are an indication that there is an open in the circuit. Technician B says excessive and unwanted circuit resistance causes the circuit's current to increase. Who is correct?

   a. Technician A
   b. Technician B
   c. Both A and B
   d. Neither A nor B

4. Why should only high-impedance meters be used on today's vehicles?

____

____

5. True or false? The current is the same throughout a series circuit. ________________

6. True or false? The computer may be damaged by using an analog meter. ________________

7. Which of the following statements is *not* true about high-resistance problems?

   a. The load in the circuit will not operate normally.
   b. The voltage drop across the load will be less than normal.
   c. The circuit's protection device will probably blow.
   d. The circuit's current will be lower than normal.

8. Technician A says fuses can be checked with a DMM. Technician B says fuses can be checked with a test light. Who is correct?

   a. Technician A
   b. Technician B
   c. Both A and B
   d. Neither A nor B

9. Technician A says the diode is open when the meter displays "OL." Technician B says most automotive diodes will drop 500 to 650 m Volts. Who is correct?

   a. Technician A
   b. Technician B
   c. Both A and B
   d. Neither A nor B

10. True or false? If circuit resistance decreases, circuit current will always increase. ________________

INFORMATION SHEET

Starting Systems Theory, Diagnosis, and Service

INFORMATION

Overview

The job of the starting system is to crank the engine. Once the engine is running, the components of the starting system are through with their job. Without the starting system, it would be difficult—if not impossible—to start a vehicle. The starting system spends less time operating than virtually any other system in the vehicle and is one of the most critical systems in vehicle operation. There are several different components to the starting system, and their service and repair are covered is this section.

Testing the Starter

There are two main circuits in every starting system: the starter circuit, and the starter control circuit. The control circuit is basically the ignition switch and assorted safety switches (such as the clutch switch and the neutral safety switch). This circuit is responsible for activating the starter circuit. The starter circuit consists of the starter motor and magnetic switch (starter relay and/or solenoid). Both of these circuits rely on the battery for power, therefore the condition of the battery and its cables affect the operation of these two circuits.

During diagnosis of starter problems, it is important to separate these two circuits. This can be done simply by checking for voltage at the starter solenoid when the ignition switch is moved to the start position. If voltage is available, the control circuit is probably working correctly. If voltage is not available to the starter circuit, then the control circuit is probably at fault.

A common cause of starter problems is high resistance in either one of these circuits or both. Often, the high resistance will cause the starter motor to overwork and go bad.

Bench Testing a Starter

With the starter removed from the vehicle, you can test individual components of the motor. Before taking apart the starter for testing, check the field coils. The field coil and frame assembly should be tested for opens and shorts to ground. These checks are done with an ohmmeter.

Set the ohmmeter on its lowest scale, then place one lead on the starter motor input terminal and the other on the insulated brushes. The ohmmeter should read zero resistance. An infinite reading indicates that there is an open in that circuit. A resistance reading of more than zero indicates resistance in that circuit. Now set the ohmmeter to the 2K scale, place one lead on the starter motor input terminal and the other on the starter motor frame. The meter should read infinite. If there is continuity, the field coils are shorted to ground. If either of these problems is found, the starter motor should be replaced.

A special tool called a "growler" is used to check motor armatures for shorts or opens. The growler produces a very strong magnetic field that is capable of inducing current flow and magnetism in a conductor.

To test the armature for shorts, place the armature in the growler and hold a thin steel blade parallel to the core. Slowly turn the armature and observe the steel blade. If the blade begins to vibrate or pull toward the core, the armature is shorted and will need to be replaced.

☐ JOB SHEET / AT 103-14

Remove, Inspect, and Replace a Starter Motor

Name ______________________ Station ______________ Date ______________

Objective

Upon completion of this job sheet, you will have demonstrated the ability to remove, inspect, and replace a starter motor. You must be able to perform these task(s) in order to pass the **ASE** test for: **Engine Performance and Electrical Systems.** Before beginning to do this Job Sheet, refer to **Chapter 18** in the AUTOMOTIVE TECHNOLOGY book for additional information.

NATEF TASKS
VI. Electrical/Electronic Systems
Category: C
Task: 4 (P-1)

Tools and Materials:

AUTOMOTIVE TECHNOLOGY 4e (Delmar Cengage Learning)

Appropriate screwdrivers	Lubricant
Appropriate wrenches	Shop towel(s)
Cleaning solvent	Service manual
Fender covers	Support brackets (if applicable)
Hoist or safety stands	Tags

Protective Gear:

Goggles or safety glasses with side shields

Describe the vehicle being worked on:

Year ________ Make ________________ Model ________________

VIN ________________ Engine type and size ________________

PROCEDURE

1. Place fender covers on the vehicle. Disconnect the battery ground cable. ☐ Task completed

   WARNING: *Never attempt to remove the starter without first disconnecting the battery.*

2. Raise and support the vehicle using a hoist or safety stands. ☐ Task completed

3. If required to access the starter, remove the front wheels. Loosen or remove the exhaust pipes and other components that block access to the starter. ☐ Task completed

4. Disconnect and tag all wires from the starter motor and/or solenoid. ☐ Task completed

5. Remove the heat shields and support brackets. Remove all mounting bolts and shims that secure the starter to the engine, and lift out the starter. ☐ Task completed

6. Visually inspect the starter bushing and armature shaft bearing area. Inspect the pinion gear and overrunning clutch drive unit. Inspect the pinion housing for cracks. If a problem is found, replace the starter motor. Record your ☐ Task completed

results on the Report Sheet for Starter Motor Inspection and Replacement, found at end of Job Sheet.

7. Check the overrunning clutch pinion clearance by either forcing (where possible) the solenoid arm to the fully applied position or by energizing the starter solenoid. ☐ Task completed

8. When the solenoid has moved the pinion to the fully engaged position, push the pinion back to remove all slack. Measure the clearance between pinion and pinion stop (Figure 6). Record the results on the Report Sheet for Starter Motor Inspection and Replacement. ☐ Task completed

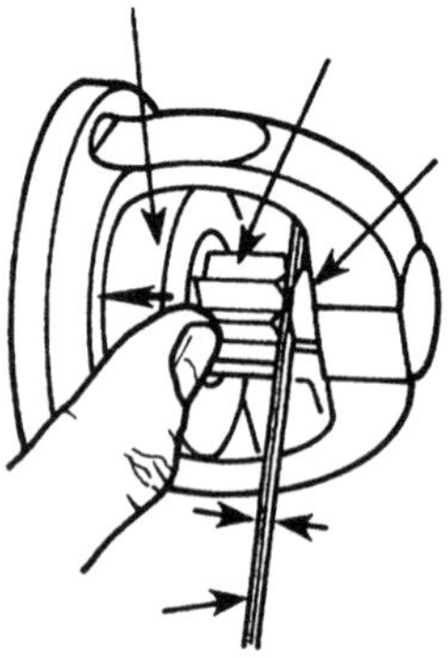

Figure 6 Measuring the clearance between the pinion gear and the pinion stop.

9. Lubricate the starter bushing and armature shaft with a few drops of 20-weight oil. ☐ Task completed

10. A shop towel, slightly dampened with clean solvent, may be used to wipe the starter housing if it is oily. If no oil is present, use a soft brush or a clean, dry rag. ☐ Task completed

11. Attach the heat shield and support brackets to the new or serviced starter motor. Some starters use a sealer in some locations to prevent entry of dust and water. When assembling parts, apply a nonhardening-type sealer. Where grommets are used, they must be in good condition and properly inserted. ☐ Task completed

12. Install the motor to the engine using all mounting bolts. Torque the bolts to specifications. ☐ Task completed

13. Check for proper flywheel engagement (Figure 7). Many starter designs have no adjustment for pinion clearance. When it is wrong, correct it by installing new parts. ☐ Task completed

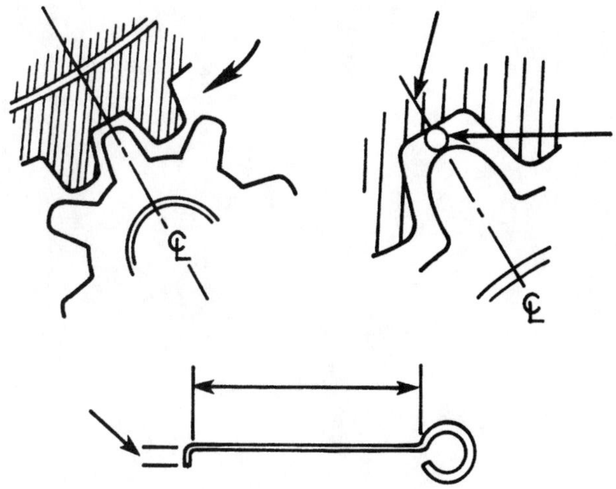

Figure 7. Checking for proper flywheel engagement.

14. Reconnect all wires to the solenoid and/or motor terminals. Remount or tighten any removed or loosened parts. ☐ Task completed

15. Lower the vehicle and reconnect the battery ground cable. Test the starter for proper operation. ☐ Task completed

16. Remove the fender covers. Clean work area, and return vehicle to designated area. ☐ Task completed

Problems Encountered

____

____

____

Instructor's Comments

____

____

____

Name ______________________________ Station ________________ Date __________________

REPORT SHEET FOR STARTER MOTOR INSPECTION AND REPLACEMENT		
	Serviceable	*Not Serviceable*
1. Visual inspection		
Bushing		
Armature shaft bearing		
Pinion gear		
Overrunning clutch		
Pinion housing		
Flywheel ring gear teeth		
	Clearance/Torque	
2. Actual pinion clearance		
3. Starter-motor-to-block-bolt torque		

Conclusions and Recommendations ____

____

____

☐ JOB SHEET / AT 103-15

Testing the Starter and Starter Circuit

Name ______________________________ Station __________________ Date __________________

Objective

Upon completion of this job sheet, you will have demonstrated the ability to check the starter circuit for excessive resistance and check the operation of the starter. You must be able to perform these task(s) in order to pass the **ASE** test for: **Engine Performance and Electrical Systems.** Before beginning to do this Job Sheet, refer to **Chapter 18** in the AUTOMOTIVE TECHNOLOGY book for additional information.

NATEF TASKS
VI. Electrical/Electronic Systems
Category: C
Task: 1 (P-1)
Task: 2 (P-1)
Category: A
Task: 9 (P-1)

Tools and Materials:

AUTOMOTIVE TECHNOLOGY 4e (Delmar Cengage Learning)
Fender covers DMM
Remote starter switch Service manual
Starting/Charging System tester (VAT-40 or similar)

Protective Gear

Goggles or safety glasses with side shields

Describe the vehicle being worked on:

Year __________ Make __________________________ Model __________________________

VIN __________________________ Engine type and size __________________________

PROCEDURE

1. Draw a simple starter circuit for the vehicle. Use the wiring diagram as a guide.

2. Place fender covers on the fenders of the vehicle. ☐ Task completed
3. Disable the ignition or fuel injection to prevent the engine from starting.

   Instructor's Check: ________________
4. If available, connect a remote starter switch. ☐ Task completed
5. Connect the voltmeter across the battery's negative cable.

   Crank the engine with the starter and observe the readings on the meter.

   Your reading was __________ volts.
6. What does this indicate?

   ____

   ____

   ____

7. Connect the voltmeter across the battery's positive cable (from battery to starter motor).

   Crank the engine with the starter and observe the readings on the meter. Your reading was _________ volts.

8. This test measured the voltage drop across everything in the positive side of the circuit. What is included in this circuit?

   ____

   ____

   ____

9. What do the test results suggest? Where should the meter be connected to next to identify the cause of any excessive voltage drop?

   ____

   ____

   ____

10. Refer to the service manual for normal starter current draw. ☐ Task completed

11. Expected starter current draw is _________ amps

    Voltage should not drop below _________ volts

12. Connect the Starting/Charging System tester cables to the vehicle. ☐ Task completed

13. Zero the ammeter on the tester. ☐ Task completed

14. Be prepared to observe the amperage when the engine begins to crank and while it is cranking. Also note the voltage when you stop cranking the engine.

    The initial current draw was _________ amps

    After _________ seconds, the current draw was _________ amps and the voltage dropped to ________ volts.

15. What is indicated by the test results? Compare your measurements to the specifications.

    ____

    ____

    ____

    ____

    ____

16. Reconnect the ignition or fuel injection system and start the engine. ☐ Task completed

Problems Encountered

____

____

____

Instructor's Comments

____

____

____

☐ JOB SHEET / AT 103-16

Control Circuit Test

Name ______________________________ Station __________________ Date __________________

Objective

Upon completion of this job sheet, you will have demonstrated the ability to properly conduct a control circuit test that examines all the wiring and components used to control the vehicle starting circuit. You must be able to perform these task(s) in order to pass the **ASE** test for: **Engine Performance and Electrical Systems.** Before beginning to do this Job Sheet, refer to **Chapter 18** in the AUTOMOTIVE TECHNOLOGY book for additional information.

Tools and Materials:

AUTOMOTIVE TECHNOLOGY 4e (Delmar Cengage Learning)

Fender covers

Service manual

Voltmeter

NATEF TASKS
VI. Electrical/Electronic Systems
Category: C
Task: 5 (P-2)

Protective Gear:

Goggles or safety glasses with side shields

Describe the vehicle being worked on:

Year __________ Make __________________________ Model __________________________

VIN __________________________ Engine type and size __________________________

PROCEDURE

1. Place fender cover on fender. Locate a vehicle wiring diagram, if possible, to identify all control circuit components. These normally include ignition switch, safety switch, starter solenoid winding, and/or a separate relay. ☐ Task completed

2. Disable the ignition or fuel injection system so the engine will not start when the starter is activated. ☐ Task completed

3. Connect the red lead of the voltmeter to the positive terminal of the battery and the black lead to the ignition switch terminal at the solenoid or starter relay. ☐ Task completed

4. Crank the engine with the starter and observe the voltage reading. Your reading was _____ volts.

5. What do you conclude from this test?

____

____

6. Normally, if you were diagnosing a system and you measured less than 0.1 volts during the last test, you would stop there and move on to testing another part of the starting system. For the purposes of this job sheet, proceed through the rest of the procedure.

7. Connect the voltmeter across the following circuits and record the voltage reading while the engine is being cranked.
   a. Battery (or fuse block) to ignition switch: ________ volts
   b. Input to output of the ignition switch: ______ volts
   c. Output of ignition switch to safety switch input: ______ volts
   d. Input of safety switch to output: _____ volts
   e. Output of safety switch to solenoid or relay: _____ volts

8. A reading of more than 0.1 volt across any one wire or switch usually indicates trouble. If a high reading is obtained across a safety switch used on automatic transmissions, check the adjustment of the switch according to manufacturer's service manual. ☐ Task completed

9. Remove fender covers. Clean work area, and return vehicle to designated area. ☐ Task completed

Problems Encountered

Instructor's Comments

CASE STUDY

A customer brings his car into the shop with a dead battery and says that every time the car gets hot and he shuts it off, he needs a jump to get it going again. The technician tests the battery and finds that it is normal. What should he check next?

☐ JOB SHEET / AT 103-17

Typical Procedure for Disassembling and Reassembling a Starter

Name ______________________ Station ______________ Date ______________

Objective

Upon completion of this job sheet, you will be able to disassemble, inspect, test, and reassemble a starter motor. You must be able to perform these task(s) in order to pass the **ASE** test for: **Electrical Systems.** Before beginning to do this Job Sheet, refer to **Chapter 18** in the AUTOMOTIVE TECHNOLOGY book for additional information.

NATEF TASKS
VI. Electrical/Electronic Systems
Category: A
Task: 12 (P-1)
Category: C
Task: 3 (P-2)

Tools and Materials:

AUTOMOTIVE TECHNOLOGY 4e (Delmar Cengage Learning)

Rags
Assorted wrenches
Snap-ring pliers
Flat blade screwdriver
Ball peen hammer
Plastic head hammer
Punch
Scribe
Small press

Protective Gear:

Goggles or safety glasses with side shields

Describe the vehicle being worked on:

Year __________ Make ______________________ Model ______________________

VIN ______________________ Engine type and size ______________________

PROCEDURE

1. With the starter motor removed, clean the case. ☐ Task completed
2. Scribe reference marks at each end of the starter end housings and the frame. ☐ Task completed
3. Disconnect the field coil connection at the solenoid. What terminal of the solenoid is this?

   ____

4. Remove the screws that attach the solenoid to the starter drive housing. ☐ Task completed
5. Rotate the solenoid until the locking flange of the solenoid is free. Then remove the solenoid. ☐ Task completed
6. Remove the through-bolts from the end frame. ☐ Task completed
7. Remove the end frame and frame of the starter. ☐ Task completed
8. Remove the armature. What did you need to do in order to get the armature out?

   ____

   ____

9. Place a deep socket over the armature shaft until it contacts the retaining ring of the starter drive. What size socket did you use?

____

10. Tap the end of the socket with a plastic-faced hammer to drive the retainer toward the armature. Move it only far enough to access the snap ring. ☐ Task completed

11. Remove the snap ring. ☐ Task completed

12. Remove the retainer from the shaft and remove the clutch and spring from the shaft. Press out the drive housing bushing and the end-frame bushing. ☐ Task completed

13. Inspect all parts and describe the condition of the following:

    Brushes: ____

    Armature: ____

    Commutator: ____

    Frame: ____

    Bearings: ____

    Starter drive: ____

    Field coils: ____

14. With an ohmmeter, check the armature for shorts, opens, and high resistance. How did you do that and what were your results?

____

____

____

____

15. With an ohmmeter, check the field windings for shorts, opens, and high resistance. How did you do that and what were your results?

____

____

____

____

16. Summarize your findings about the parts of the starter. What parts can be reused? What parts need to be replaced?

____

____

____

____

17. Gather all of the required new parts, then press in the drive housing bushing and the end-frame bushing, using the appropriate drivers. ☐ Task completed

18. Install the clutch and spring onto the armature shaft and install the retainer. ☐ Task completed

19. Place the deep socket over the armature shaft until it contacts the retaining ring of the starter drive. Tap the end of the socket with a plastic-faced hammer to drive the retainer toward the armature. Move it only far enough to install a new snap ring. ☐ Task completed

20. Install the armature into the frame. What did you need to do in order to get the armature in?

____

____

21. Install the end frame over the armature shaft. Make sure the brushes are in contact with the commutator. Also make sure the end frame is aligned with the alignment marks you made during disassembly. What did you need to do in order to get the commutator past the brushes?

____

____

____

22. Install and tighten the through-bolts from the end frame. ☐ Task completed

23. Rotate the solenoid until it is locked in place. ☐ Task completed

24. Install and tighten the screws that attach the solenoid to the starter drive housing. ☐ Task completed

25. Reconnect the field coil connection at the solenoid. ☐ Task completed

26. Bench test the starter. How did you do that and what were the results?

____

____

____

Problems Encountered

____

____

____

Instructor's Comments

____

____

____

REVIEW QUESTIONS

1. True or false? Clean battery cable connections are an important part of proper starter motor operation.

   ____

2. Technician A says a faulty starter solenoid could cause the starter motor not to work. Technician B says a bad ground cable could cause the starter motor not to work. Who is correct?

   a. Technician A
   b. Technician B
   c. Both A and B
   d. Neither A nor B

3. True or false? An ohmmeter is used to check the starter circuit. ____________________

4. True or false? A voltmeter can be used to check the starter circuit. ____________________

5. Technician A says that a bad ground connection at the battery can cause the starter motor to draw higher than normal amounts of current. Technician B says a bad connection at the battery's positive terminal will reduce the amount of voltage available at the starter. Who is correct?

   a. Technician A
   b. Technician B
   c. Both A and B
   d. Neither A nor B

6. Technician A says an infinite reading on an ohmmeter connected across two segments of an armature's commutator means the armature windings are shorted. Technician B says an ohmmeter reading of zero when the leads are connected from the core or shaft of the armature to a segment of the commutator means the armature windings are okay. Who is correct?

   a. Technician A
   b. Technician B
   c. Both A and B
   d. Neither A nor B

7. Technician A says that when the starter motor spins but the solenoid does not engage the engine's flywheel, the starter control circuit has a fault. Technician B says there will be higher than normal current draw by the starter if the motor does not spin as fast as it should. Who is correct?

   a. Technician A
   b. Technician B
   c. Both A and B
   d. Neither A nor B

8. List four major components of the starting circuit.

   a. ____________________
   b. ____________________
   c. ____________________
   d. ____________________

9. Where is a starter motor typically grounded?

   ____

   ____

10. Describe the function the neutral safety switch plays in the starter circuit.

    ____

    ____

INFORMATION SHEET

Charging Systems: Theory, Diagnosis, and Service

INFORMATION

Overview

The charging system must maintain enough voltage to keep the battery charged,, even when running at its rated amperage output.

Charging Systems

The heart of the charging system is the Ac generator (alternator). The rotor of the generator is driven by the engine's crankshaft via the drive belt(s). The rotor becomes a rotating magnetic field. It rotates inside the stator winding assembly. As the magnetic field moves past the windings, AaC voltage is induced in the windings. This AC voltage is changed to a pulsating DC voltage, which is used to recharge the battery and to power the vehicles accessories.

Some form of regulation is used to keep the generator from providing excessive aounts of votage. This regulation may be handled by the vehicle's computer or by a separate voltage regulator. Most voltage regulators are mounted inside or out side of the generator. Others are mounted away from the generator.

Safety Precautions

- Before beginning any work on the charging or starting system, keep the following safety precautions in mind:
- Disconnect the battery ground cable before removing any leads from the system. Do not reconnect the ground cable until all wiring connections have been made.
- Avoid contact with the generator output terminal. This terminal is always hot when the battery is connected.
- Always make sure the ignition switch is in the off position, except during test procedures directing otherwise.
- When installing the battery, be careful to observe the correct polarity. Reversing the cable will destroy the diodes. Proper polarity must be observed when connecting a booster battery.
- Never operate a generator with an open circuit (with generator or regulator lead disconnected). This situation will allow the generator to build up very high voltage, which could damage the diodes.
- When soldering the rectifier (diode) lead, always grasp the lead with a pair of pliers between the joint and the rectifier body. The pliers will act as a heat sink and protect the rectifier from overheating.
- Unless directed to do so by the service manual, never ground the field circuit.
- Remove the battery ground connection before removing or replacing system wires or units. This is also necessary before connecting test instruments other than a voltmeter. An accidental short at the generator, regulator, or elsewhere can damage the test unit or components.

- Disconnect the connector plug from the regulator before removing the mounting screws. Pulling the connector from an ungrounded regulator can ruin it.
- Keep the carbon pile of test equipment off at all times, except during the actual test procedure.
- Make sure all hair, clothing, and jewelry are kept away from moving parts.
- Metallic jewelry should not be worn when working around electrical circuits. An accidental circuit path could result in serious injury and/or property damage.

☐ JOB SHEET / AT 103-18

Visually Inspecting a Charging System

Name ______________________ Station ______________ Date ______________

Objective

Upon completion of this job sheet, you will have demonstrated the ability to visually inspect the components of a charging system. You must be able to perform these task(s) in order to pass the **ASE** test for: **Electrical Systems.** Before beginning to do this Job Sheet, refer to **Chapter 19** in the AUTOMOTIVE TECHNOLOGY book for additional information.

Tools and Materials:

AUTOMOTIVE TECHNOLOGY 4e (Delmar Cengage Learning)

Belt tension gauge

Service manual

NATEF TASKS
VI. Electrical/Electronic Systems
Category: D
Task: 3 (P-2)

Protective Gear:

Goggles or safety glasses with side shields

Describe the vehicle being worked on:

Year ________ Make ______________ Model ______________

VIN ______________ Engine type and size ______________

PROCEDURE

1. Inspect the condition of the drive belt. Describe your findings:

____

____

2. Look up the drive belt tension specification in the service manual. ☐ Task completed

3. Using a belt tension gauge, measure the tension of the generator's drive belt and describe your findings:

____

____

4. Visually inspect the battery and battery cables and describe their condition:

____

____

5. Visually inspect the wires connected to the generator and regulator and describe their condition:

____

____

6. Start the engine and listen for noisy belts, bad generator bearings, and bad diodes (a whirring sound). Describe what you heard:

   ____

   ____

Problems Encountered

____

____

____

Instructor's Comments

____

____

____

☐ JOB SHEET / AT 103-19

Inspect, Replace, and Adjust Drive Belts and Pulleys

Name ______________________ Station ______________ Date ______________

Objective

Upon completion of this job sheet, you will have demonstrated the ability to inspect, replace, and adjust drive belts and pulleys. You must be able to perform these task(s) in order to pass the **ASE** test for: **Electrical Systems.** Before beginning to do this Job Sheet, refer to **Chapter 19** in the AUTOMOTIVE TECHNOLOGY book for additional information.

Tools and Materials:

AUTOMOTIVE TECHNOLOGY 4e (Delmar Cengage Learning)

Two vehicles, one with a serpentine belt and the other with V-belts

Service manuals for the above vehicles

Belt tension gauge

Hand tools

NATEF TASKS
VI. Electrical/Electronic Systems
Category: D
Task: 3 (P-2)

Protective Gear:

Goggles or safety glasses with side shields

Describe the vehicle being worked on:

Year __________ Make ____________________ Model ____________________

VIN ____________________ Engine type and size ____________________

PROCEDURE

1. On the vehicle with a serpentine belt, carefully inspect the belt and describe the general condition of the belt.

____

____

____

2. With the proper belt tension gauge, check the tension of the belt. Belt tension should be ______________ . You found ______________.

3. Based on the above, what are your recommendations?

____

____

4. Describe the procedure for adjusting the tension of the belt:

____

____

5. Referring to the service manual, describe the procedure for removing the belt:

____

____

6. Draw the proper routing for installing a new drive belt:

7. On the vehicle with V-belts, you will find more than one drive belt. List the different belts by their purpose.

____

____

____

8. Carefully inspect the belts and describe the general condition of each one.

____

____

____

9. Inspect the tension of the AC generator drive belt. Belt tension should be ______________. You found ______________.

10. Based on the above, what are your recommendations?

____

____

11. Describe the procedure for adjusting the tension of the belt:

____

____

____

12. Describe the procedure for removing an AC generator drive belt:

____

____

____

Problems Encountered

____

____

____

Instructor's Comments

____

____

____

☐ JOB SHEET / AT 103-20

Remove and Replace an AC Generator

Name ______________________ Station ______________ Date ______________

Objective

Upon completion of this job sheet, you will have demonstrated the ability to remove a generator from a vehicle and install a generator on the vehicle. You must be able to perform these task(s) in order to pass the **ASE** test for: **Engine Performance and Electrical Systems.** Before beginning to do this Job Sheet, refer to **Chapter 19** in the AUTOMOTIVE TECHNOLOGY book for additional information.

Tools and Materials:

AUTOMOTIVE TECHNOLOGY 4e (Delmar Cengage Learning)

Appropriate wrenches — Screwdrivers

Fender cover — Service manual

NATEF TASKS
VI. Electrical/Electronic Systems
Category: D
Task: 4 (P-1)

Protective Gear:

Goggles or safety glasses with side shields

Describe the vehicle being worked on:

Year ________ Make ____________________ Model ____________________

VIN ____________________ Engine type and size ____________________

PROCEDURE (REMOVING GENERATOR)

1. Place fender covers on the fenders. Disconnect the negative (–) battery cable first and then the positive (+) battery cable at the battery. ☐ Task completed

   WARNING: *Never attempt to remove the generator without isolating the battery first.*

2. Disconnect the wiring leads from the generator. ☐ Task completed
3. Following the appropriate procedures, loosen the adjusting bolts and move the generator to provide sufficient slack to remove the generator drive belts. ☐ Task completed
4. Remove the through-bolts that retain the generator. ☐ Task completed
5. Remove the generator from the vehicle. ☐ Task completed

PROCEDURE (INSTALLING GENERATOR)

1. Install the generator onto its mounting bracket with bolts, washers, and nuts. Do not tighten. ☐ Task completed
2. Install the generator drive belts and tighten them to the proper belt tension. ☐ Task completed

   Specification ________________________________

3. Tighten all bolts to the specified torque. ☐ Task completed

   Specification ______________________________

4. Install the generator terminal plug and battery leads to the unit. ☐ Task completed

5. Connect the negative battery cable. ☐ Task completed

6. Test the generator for specified output and record: ☐ Task completed

   Specification ______________________________

   Actual ______________________________

   If the output is okay, remove the fender covers.

Problems Encountered

____

____

____

Instructor's Comments

____

____

____

☐ JOB SHEET / AT 103-21

Charging System Testing

Name ______________________ Station ______________ Date ______________

Objective

Upon completion of this job sheet, you will have demonstrated the ability to test the operation of the charging system. You must be able to perform these task(s) in order to pass the **ASE** test for: **Electrical Systems.** Before beginning to do this Job Sheet, refer to **Chapter 19** in the AUTOMOTIVE TECHNOLOGY book for additional information.

NATEF TASKS
VI. Electrical/Electronic Systems
Category: D
Task: 1 (P-1)
Task: 2 (P-1)
Task: 5 (P-1)

Tools and Materials:

AUTOMOTIVE TECHNOLOGY 4e (Delmar Cengage Learning)
Service manual and wiring diagram for the vehicle
DMM
Starting/Charging System tester (VAT-40 or similar)

Protective Gear:

Goggles or safety glasses with side shields

Describe the vehicle being worked on:

Year ________ Make ____________________ Model ____________________

VIN ____________________ Engine type and size ____________________

PROCEDURE

1. Describe the general appearance of the AC generator and the wires that are attached to it.

____

____

____

____

2. Measure the open circuit voltage of the battery. Your measurement was _______ volts.

3. From the wiring diagram, identify the output, input, and ground wires for the AC generator. Describe these wires, by color and location, below.

____

____

____

____

4. Start the engine and allow it to run. Then turn on the headlights in the high-beam mode. ☐ Task completed

5. Connect the DMM across the charging system's output wire. Measure the voltage drop and record your readings.

____

6. Connect the DMM across the charging system's input wire. Measure the voltage drop and record your readings.

____

7. Connect the DMM across the charging system's ground wire. Measure the voltage drop and record your readings.

____

8. Based on the above tests, what is indicated by the results?

____

____

____

____

9. Identify the type and model of AC generator. What type is it?

____

What are the output specifications for this AC generator?

_________ amps and _________ volts at ___________ rpm

10. Connect the Starting/Charging System tester to the vehicle. ☐ Task completed

11. Start the engine and run it at the specified engine speed. ☐ Task completed

12. Observe the output to the battery. The meter readings are:

__________ amps and ________ volts

13. Compare readings to specifications and give recommendations.

____

____

____

____

14. If readings are outside of the specifications, refer to the service manual to find the proper way to full field the AC generator. Describe the method.

____

____

____

____

15. Full field the generator and observe the output to the battery. The meter readings are:

    __________ amps and ________ volts

16. Compare readings to specifications and give recommendations.

    ____

    ____

    ____

    ____

    ____

Problems Encountered

____

____

____

Instructor's Comments

____

____

____

☐ JOB SHEET / AT 103-22

Checking the Voltage Regulator

Name ______________________ Station ______________ Date ______________

Objective

Upon completion of this job sheet, you will be able to inspect and test a voltage regulator/regulation circuit. You must be able to perform these task(s) in order to pass the **ASE** test for: **Electrical and Electronic Systems.** Before beginning to do this Job Sheet, refer to **Chapter 19** in the AUTOMOTIVE TECHNOLOGY book for additional information.

Tools and Materials:

AUTOMOTIVE TECHNOLOGY 4e (Delmar Cengage Learning)

DMM

Tachometer

Protective Gear:

Goggles or safety glasses with side shields

NATEF TASKS
VI. Electrical/Electronic Systems
Category: A
Task: 2 (P-1)
Task: 5 (P-1)
Category: E
Task: 1 (P-1)

Describe the vehicle being worked on:

Year ________ Make ____________________ Model ____________________

VIN ____________________ Engine type and size ____________________

PROCEDURE

1. Check the alignment, condition, and tension of the generator's drive belt. Describe your findings.

   ____

   ____

2. Inspect the battery and the cables and terminals connected to it. Describe your findings.

   ____

   ____

3. Inspect all charging system wiring and connectors. Describe your findings.

   ____

   ____

4. Inspect the AC generator and regulator mountings for loose or missing bolts. ☐ Task completed

5. Connect a voltmeter across the battery terminals. ☐ Task completed

6. Connect a tachometer if the vehicle doesn't have one. ☐ Task completed

7. With the engine off, measure and record the voltage at the battery. Describe your findings.

____

____

8. Start the engine and bring its speed to about 1500 to 2000 rpm. ☐ Task completed

9. Measure and record the voltage at the battery. It should now be 13.5 to 14.5 volts. Describe your findings.

____

____

10. If the charging voltage was too high, describe what may be the cause.

____

____

11. If the charging voltage was too low, describe what may be the cause.

____

____

12. Explain how this test checks the operation of the voltage regulator.

____

____

____

Problems Encountered

____

____

____

Instructor's Comments

____

____

____

☐ JOB SHEET / AT 103-23

AC Generator Disassembly and Assembly

Name ______________________ Station ______________ Date ______________

Objective

Upon completion of this job sheet, you will have demonstrated the ability to properly disassemble and assemble an AC generator. You must be able to perform these task(s) in order to pass the **ASE** test for: **Electrical Systems.** Before beginning to do this Job Sheet, refer to **Chapter 19** in the AUTOMOTIVE TECHNOLOGY book for additional information.

NATEF TASKS
VI. Electrical/Electronic Systems
Category: D
Task: 4 (P-1)

Tools and Materials:

AUTOMOTIVE TECHNOLOGY 4e (Delmar Cengage Learning)

400-grain polishing cloth
Appropriate wrenches and screwdrivers
Clean shop towel(s)
Cleaning solvent
Fender cover
High-temperature bearing grease
Press
Pulley puller
Screwdrivers
Scriber
Service manual
Small pry bar

Protective Gear:

Goggles or safety glasses with side shields

Describe the type of vehicle the generator was on:

Year ________ Make ____________________ Model ____________________

VIN ____________________ Engine type and size ____________________

Describe the type of generator:

____

PROCEDURE (DISASSEMBLY)

1. Place fender covers on the fenders. Disconnect the negative battery cable. ☐ Task completed

   WARNING: *Never attempt to disconnect the generator harness without first disconnecting the battery.*

2. Disconnect the battery positive cable and disconnect the wiring from the alternator. ☐ Task completed

3. Remove the generator from the vehicle. ☐ Task completed

4. Following the appropriate procedure, remove the brush assembly. ☐ Task completed

   CAUTION: *Do not attempt to remove the pulley by prying it off.*

5. Remove the through-bolts. Mark the housing halves with a scriber. Pry the slip ring end frame and drive end frame apart, using a suitable small pry bar. Separate the units. Make sure the stator is pulled with the rear half. ☐ Task completed

PROCEDURE (ASSEMBLY)

1. Assemble in the reverse order of disassembly. Work carefully. Make sure all parts are correctly located. Align the scribe marks. If press fit is required, use a press. ☐ Task completed
2. Reassemble the brush unit. Some generator brush assembly designs permit the use of a pin to hold the brushes in the holder during assembly. Some require hooking the brush leads over a section of the brush holder for installation. Another type uses simple brush holders that permit installation after the generator is assembled. If a brush holder pin is used, or if the leads are hooked, remove the pin or straighten them after assembly. ☐ Task completed
3. Spin the rotor to check for free operation. ☐ Task completed
4. When mounting the generator to the engine, adjust the belt tension by prying on the edge of the heavy drive end frame. Never pry against the center or at the slip ring frame end. Tighten the belt to its tension specification and torque the bolts to specification. ☐ Task completed
5. Connect all wires to the generator. Connect the positive (+) battery cable first, then the negative (–) cable. ☐ Task completed
6. Start the engine and test the charging system. ☐ Task completed
7. Remove fender cover. ☐ Task completed

Problems Encountered

____

____

____

Instructor's Comments

____

____

____

☐ JOB SHEET / AT 103-24

Inspect, Clean, and Test AC Generator Components

Name ______________________ Station ______________ Date ______________

Objective

Upon completion of this job sheet, you will have demonstrated the ability to inspect, clean, test, repair, and replace various components of a generator. You must be able to perform these task(s) in order to pass the **ASE** test for: **Electrical Systems.** Before beginning to do this Job Sheet, refer to **Chapter 19** in the AUTOMOTIVE TECHNOLOGY book for additional information.

Tools and Materials:

AUTOMOTIVE TECHNOLOGY 4e (Delmar Cengage Learning)

400-grain polishing cloth

Hand tools

Clean shop towel(s)

High-temperature bearing grease

Ohmmeter

Press

Soldering iron

Solder

Service manual

NATEF TASKS
VI. Electrical/Electronic Systems
Category: D
Task: 4 (P-1)

Protective Gear:

Goggles or safety glasses with side shields

Describe the type of vehicle the generator was on:

Year ________ Make ____________________ Model ____________________

VIN ____________________ Engine type and size ____________________

Describe the type of generator:

____

PROCEDURE (INSPECT AND CLEAN)

1. Wipe the stator, rotor, and front bearing with a clean cloth. Do not clean these parts with solvent. ☐ Task completed

2. Rotate the front bearing on the drive end of the rotor shaft. Check for any scraping noise, looseness, or roughness. Look for excessive lubricant leakage. If any of these conditions exist, replace the bearing. Pack the bearings with high-temperature bearing grease where required. Record your results on the Report Sheet for Inspection and Cleaning Generator Components, found at the end of Job Sheet. ☐ Task completed

3. Inspect the rotor shaft rear bearing surface for roughness or severe chatter marks. Replace the rotor assembly if the shaft is not smooth. Record your results on the Reports Sheet for Inspection and Cleaning Generator Components. ☐ Task completed

4. Place the rear bearing on the slip ring end of the rotor shaft and rotate the bearing. Make the same check for noise, looseness, and roughness as was made for the front bearing. Inspect the rollers and cage for damage. Replace the rear bearing if these conditions exist or if lubricant is lost or contaminated. Record your results on the Report Sheet for Inspection and Cleaning Generator Components. ☐ Task completed

5. Inspect the slip rings for nicks and scratches. These may be removed by turning the slip rings while holding 400-grain polishing cloth against them. (Never use emery cloth.) If the rings are badly damaged, replace the rotor assembly. Record your results on the Report Sheet for Inspection and Cleaning Generator Components. ☐ Task completed

6. Inspect all wire leads on both the rotor and stator assemblies for loose or broken connections. Check the windings for burned insulation. Replace all parts that show signs of burned insulation. Record your results on the Report Sheet for Inspection and Cleaning Generator Components. ☐ Task completed

7. Inspect the pulley and fan for excessive looseness on the rotor shaft and for cracks or other damage. Replace any pulley or fan that is loose, cracked, or bent out of shape. Record your results on the Report Sheet for Inspection and Cleaning Generator Components. ☐ Task completed

8. Inspect both the front and rear housing for cracks, particularly in webbed areas at the mounting ear. Replace a damaged or cracked housing. Record your results on the Report Sheet for Inspection and Cleaning Generator Components. ☐ Task completed

9. Wipe all grease from the rectifier assembly base and rectifier mounting areas of the rear housing with a clean shop towel. ☐ Task completed

10. Brushes must be free of any oil or grease. Replace the brushes if they are worn shorter than one-fourth inch. ☐ Task completed

Problems Encountered

____

____

____

Instructor's Comments

____

____

____

Name ______________________ Station ______________ Date ______________

REPORT SHEET FOR INSPECTION AND CLEANING GENERATOR COMPONENTS		
	Serviceable	*Corrective Action*
1. Visual inspection		
Front bearing		
Rotor shaft		
Rear bearing		
Slip rings		
Wire leads		
Windings		
Pulley		
Front housing		
Rear housing		
Brushes		
Conclusions and Recommendations ______________________		

PROCEDURE (FIELD OPEN OR SHORT-CIRCUIT TEST)

1. With the generator removed from the vehicle but not disassembled, identify the positive and negative terminals on the generator. Connect an ohmmeter across these two terminals (Figure 8). Then spin the generator pulley with your hand. ☐ Task completed

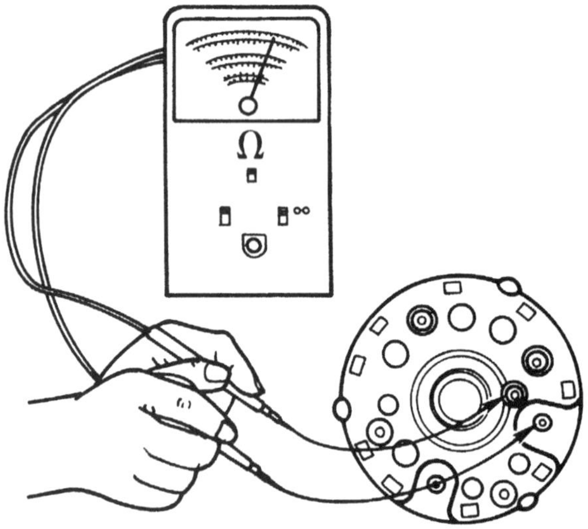

Figure 8. Connections for checking the field coil with an ohmmeter.

The ohmmeter reading should be between 2.5 and 100 ohms and should fluctuate while the pulley is turning. Record the results on the Report Sheet for Generator Components Tests found at end of Job Sheet. An infinite reading (no meter movement) indicates an open brush lead, worn or stuck brushes, or a bad rotor assembly. An ohmmeter reading less than 2.5 ohms indicates a shorted brush assembly, shorted field terminal, or bad rotor.

PROCEDURE (STATOR COIL GROUNDED TEST)

1. Disassemble the generator to expose the stator coil. ☐ Task completed
2. Connect the ohmmeter probes to one of the stator leads and to the stator's laminated core. Be sure the probe makes a good electrical connection with the stator core. Meter should show infinite reading (no meter movement). ☐ Task completed

   Repeat this test for each stator lead. Do not touch the metal probes or stator leads with your hands. Contact will result in an incorrect reading. Record results on the Report Sheet for Generator Component Tests, found at end of Job Sheet.

   If the meter does not indicate an infinite reading (needle moves), the stator winding is shorted to the core and must be replaced.

PROCEDURE (STATOR COIL OPEN TEST)

1. Connect an ohmmeter across two of the stator leads. Record your measurement on the Report Sheet for Generator Component Tests, found at end of Job Sheet. ☐ Task completed

2. Repeat this test on the other stator leads to be sure that you have tested all combinations. Some resistance should be measured across all combinations of stator leads. If an infinite reading is observed, the stator is replaced. ☐ Task completed

PROCEDURE (ROTOR OPEN OR SHORT-CIRCUIT TEST)

1. Contact each ohmmeter probe to a different rotor slip ring. The meter reading should be approximately 2.0–3.5 ohms. (Check the service manual.) A higher reading indicates a damaged slip ring solder connection or a broken wire. A lower reading indicates a shorted wire or slip ring. Replace the rotor if it is damaged and cannot be serviced. ☐ Task completed

2. Contact one ohmmeter probe to a slip ring and the other probe to the rotor shaft. The meter reading should be infinite (no deflection). Record the results on the Report Sheet for Generator Component Tests, found at end of Job Sheet. A reading other than infinite indicates the rotor is shorted to the shaft. Inspect the slip ring soldered terminals to ensure that they are not bent and not touching the rotor shaft, or that excess solder is not shorting the rotor coil connections to the shaft. Replace the rotor if it is shorted and cannot be serviced. ☐ Task completed

PROCEDURE (DIODE TEST)

CAUTION: *Digital meters cannot be used to perform the following diode tests, unless the DMM has a diode test mode.*

1. To test one set of diodes, contact one probe to the terminal bolt and contact each of the three stator lead terminals with the other probe (Figure 9). Reverse the probes and repeat the test. All diodes should show a low reading of approximately 6 ohms in one direction and an infinite reading (no needle movement) with the probes reversed. The low reading may vary with the type of meter used. This reading may be checked against a good rectifier, if available. Record the results on the Report Sheet for Generator Component Tests, found at end of Job Sheet. ☐ Task completed

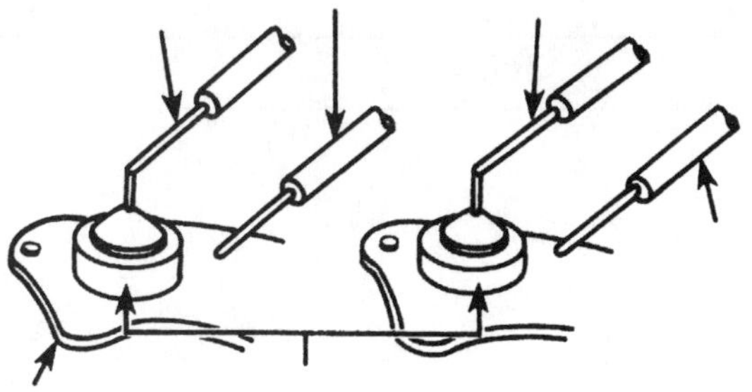

Figure 9. Testing one set of diodes with an ohmmeter.

2. Repeat the preceding tests for the other set of diodes using the other terminal screw. If the meter readings are not as specified, replace the rectifier assembly. In some charging systems, all three diodes are grouped in the same dielectric case. If one of the diodes tests faulty, the entire unit must be replaced. ☐ Task completed

PROCEDURE (REPLACING A DIODE)

1. When soldering the replacement diode leads, always grip the lead, between the diode and the soldered area, with a pair of pliers (Figure 10). The pliers will protect the diode from excessive heat. ☐ Task completed

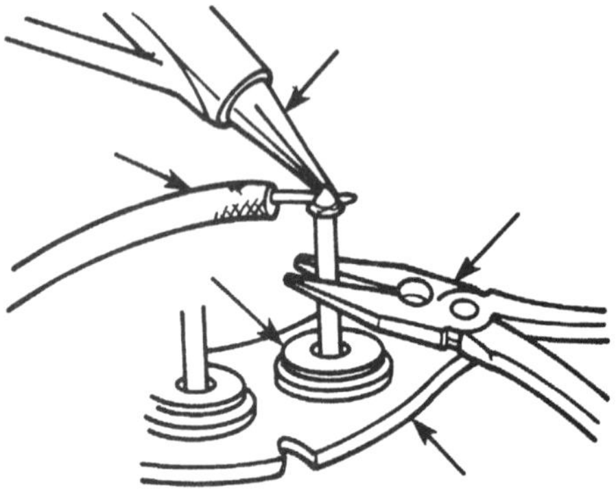

Figure 10. Soldering the replacement diode's leads.

2. After proper corrective action has been taken for all generator components, reassemble the generator. ☐ Task completed

Problems Encountered

____

____

____

Instructor's Comments

____

____

____

Name ______________________ Station ______________ Date ______________

REPORT SHEET FOR GENERATOR COMPONENT TESTS	
1. Field circuit test	
Open	
Short	
2. Stator coil grounded test	
Ohmmeter reading	
Serviceable	
Nonserviceable	
3. Stator coil open test	
Ohmmeter readings	
Serviceable	
Nonserviceable	
4. Rotor tests	
a. Specifications	
Ohmmeter reading	
b. Slip ring to shaft	
Ohmmeter reading	
5. Diode test	
Serviceable	
Nonserviceable	

Conclusions and Recommendations ______________________________________

____

____

CASE STUDIES

Case Study 1

The battery on a customer's car seems always to overcharge. The battery seems very hot after operation, and the customer has replaced the battery once. What could be the problem?

Case Study 2

The customer complains that the generator light is on constantly when the engine is running. What could be the problem?

REVIEW QUESTIONS

1. How should a diode be tested? ______________________________

____

2. When cleaning the generator, what parts must not be cleaned in solvent?

____

3. Test the armature for______________________________

and ______________________________.

4. Always ______________ the battery ______________ before connecting or disconnecting any wire at the generator.

5. What effect does a shorted diode have on a generator's output? ______________

____

6. True or false? The regulator in a typical charging system controls current and voltage output._____

____

7. Technician A says AC voltage is present at the stator leads in a generator. Technician B says the output from a generator is pulsating DC voltage. Who is correct?

a. Technician A
b. Technician B
c. Both A and B
d. Neither A nor B

8. Technician A says that when checking a diode with an ohmmeter, continuity in both directions across the diode indicates that it is a good diode. Technician B says that when an ohmmeter is connected across the two slip rings of a rotor, a low reading indicates that the rotor is shorted. Who is correct?

a. Technician A
b. Technician B
c. Both A and B
d. Neither A nor B

9. True or false? An AC generator changes mechanical energy into electrical energy through principles of magnetic induction. ______________________________

10. The rotor should be inspected for______________________________

and ______________________________.

INFORMATION SHEET

Lighting Systems

INFORMATION

Overview

Every automotive vehicle is equipped with various lighting systems. They include marker lights, headlights, taillights, parking lights, dome light(s), hazard warning lights, instrument lights, cornering lights, and other convenience lights.

Lighting System Diagnosis and Testing

Before performing any lighting system tests, make sure the battery is fully charged and in good condition. Be sure all battery cable connections are clean and tight. A visual inspection is part of diagnosing the lighting system. Check the wires for frayed or damaged insulation, loose connections, or improper harness routing. Refer to the vehicle's wiring diagram.

Any problems found during the visual inspection should be corrected before further diagnostics are performed.

Table 1. Lighting System Diagnosis.

Symptom	*Possible Cause*	*Remedy*
Hazard flasher lamps do not flash.	Fuse or circuit breaker burned out	Replace fuse or circuit breaker. If fuse or circuit breaker blows again, check for short circuit.
	Worn or damaged hazard flasher unit	Substitute a flasher known to be good. Replace flasher, if damaged.
	Worn or damaged turn-signal switch	Repair or replace turn-signal switch.
	Open circuit in wiring	Repair, as required.
	Worn or damaged hazard flasher switch	Repair or replace turn-signal switch and wiring assembly, which includes hazard flasher switch.
Backup lamps—one lamp does not function.	Bulb burned out	Replace bulb.
	Loose wiring connections	Secure connections, where accessible.
	Open circuit in wiring	Repair, as required.
Backup lamps—both lamps do not function.	Fuse or circuit breaker burned out	Replace fuse or circuit breaker. If fuse or circuit breaker blows again, check for short circuit.
	Backup lamp switch out of adjustment	Adjust switch.

(continued)

Table 1. Continued

Symptom	*Possible Cause*	*Remedy*
	Worn or damaged backup lamp switch	Replace switch.
	Loose wiring connections	Secure connections, where accessible.
	Open wiring or poor ground	Repair, as required.
	Bulbs burned out	Replace bulb.
Instrument panel lamp does not light.	Bulb burned out	Replace bulb.
	Fuse burned out	Replace fuse.
	Open circuit in wiring, rheostat, or printed-circuit board	Inspect for short circuit. Repair, as required.
Dome lamp does not come on when door is opened.	Connector loose	Secure or replace.
	Blown fuse	Replace fuse. If fuse blows again, check for short circuit.
	Bulb burned out	Replace bulb.
	Open circuit in wiring	Repair, as required.
	Worn or damaged door jamb switch	Replace switch.
Dome lamp stays on.	Worn or damaged door jamb switch	Replace switch.
	Worn or damaged main lighting switch	Replace main lighting.
Map lamp does not come on when switch is actuated.	Bulb burned out	Replace bulb.
	Blown fuse	Replace fuse.
	Open circuit in wiring	Repair, as required.
	Worn or damaged switch in lamp circuit	Replace lamp assembly.
Map lamp stays on.	Worn or damaged switch in lamp circuit	Replace lamp assembly.
Side or roof marker lamp does not light.	Bulb burned out	Replace bulb.
	Open circuit or poor ground	Inspect bulb socket for corrosion and good ground. Repair, as required.
Turn-signal lamps do not light.	Fuse or circuit breaker burned out	Replace fuse or circuit breaker. If fuse or circuit breaker blows again, check for short circuit.

Table 1. Continued

Symptom	*Possible Cause*	*Remedy*
	Worn or damaged turn-signal flasher	Substitute a known good flasher. Replace, if required.
	Loose wiring connections	Secure connections, where accessible.
	Open circuit or poor ground	Repair, as required.
	Damaged turn-signal switch	Verify continuity of switch assembly. Replace turn-signal switch and wiring assembly, as necessary.
Turn-signal lamps light but do not flash.	Worn or damaged turn-signal flasher	Substitute a known good flasher. Replace, if required.
	Poor ground	Repair ground.
Front turn-signal lamps do not light.	Loose wiring connector or open circuit	Repair wiring, as required.
Rear turn-signal lamps do not light.	Loose wiring connector or open circuit	Repair wiring, as required.
One turn-signal lamp does not light.	Bulb burned out	Replace bulb.
	Open circuit or poor ground	
Headlights do not light.	Loose wiring connections	Test and secure connections at headlight switch and dash panel connector.
	Open circuit in wiring	Test power to and from headlight switch. Repair as necessary.
	Worn or damaged headlight switch	Verify condition. Replace headlight switch, if necessary.
One headlight does not work.	Loose wiring connections	Secure connections to headlight and ground.
	Sealed-beam bulb burned out	Replace bulb.
	Corroded socket	Repair or replace, as required.
All headlights out; park and taillights are okay.	Loose wiring connections	Test and secure connections at dimmer switch and headlight switch.
	Worn or damaged dimmer switch	Verify dimmer switch operation. Inspect for corroded connector. Replace, if required.
	Worn or damaged headlight switch	Verify condition. Replace headlight switch, as necessary.

(continued)

Table 1. Continued

Symptom	Possible Cause	Remedy
	Open circuit in wiring or poor ground	Repair, if required.
Both low-beam or both high-beam headlights do not work.	Loose wiring connections	Test and secure connection at dimmer switch and headlight switch.
	Worn or damaged dimmer switch	Test dimmer switch operation. Inspect for corroded connector. Replace, if required.
	Open circuit or poor ground	Repair.
One taillight out.	Bulb burned out	Replace bulb.
	Open wiring or poor ground	Repair as necessary.
	Corroded bulb socket	Repair or replace socket.
All taillights and marker lamps out; headlights okay.	Loose wiring connections	Secure wiring connections, where accessible.
	Open wiring or poor ground	Verify the operation of front park and marker lamps. Repair as necessary.
	Blown fuse	Replace fuse.
	Damaged headlight switch	Verify condition. Replace headlight switch, if necessary.
Stop lights do not work.	Fuse or circuit breaker burned out	Replace fuse or circuit breaker. If fuse or circuit breaker blows again, check for short circuit.
	Worn or damaged turn-signal switch	Inspect turn-signal switch operation. Replace if necessary.
	Loose wiring connections	Secure connection at stop-light switch.
	Worn or damaged stop-light switch	Replace switch.
	Open circuit or poor ground	Repair as required.
Stop lights stay on continuously.	Damaged stop-light switch	Disconnect wiring connector from switch. If lamp goes out, replace switch.
	Switch out of adjustment	Adjust switch.
	Short circuit in wiring	If lamp stays on, check for a short circuit. Repair as necessary.
One parking lamp out.	Bulb burned out	Replace bulb.
	Open wiring or poor ground	Repair as necessary.
	Corroded bulb socket	Repair or replace socket.
All parking lamps out.	Loose wiring connections	Secure wiring connections.
	Open wiring or poor ground	Repair as necessary.
	Bad switch	Replace switch.

☐ JOB SHEET / AT 103-25

Using Wiring Schematics

Name ______________________ Station ______________ Date ______________

Objective

Upon completion of this job sheet, you will demonstrate the ability to diagnose common electrical system problems using a wiring diagram. You must be able to perform these task(s) in order to pass the **ASE** test for: **Electrical Systems.**

Tools and Materials:

AUTOMOTIVE TECHNOLOGY 4e (Delmar Cengage Learning)

Instructor Notes

Protective Gear:

N/A

NATEF TASKS
VI. Electrical/Electronic Systems
Category: A
Task: 1 (P-1)

PROCEDURE

1. Below is a typical headlight wiring schematic. Trace through the schematic and label the hot, ground, load, protection and control devices. ☐ Task completed

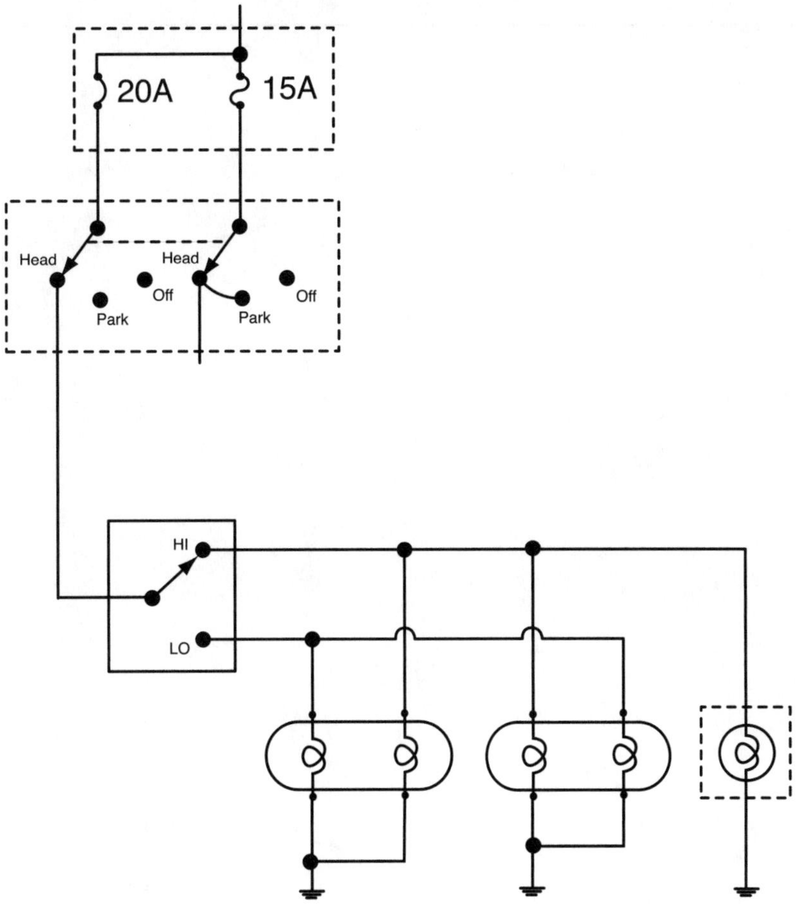

2. A customer complains that his cigar lighter does not pop out or become hot. However, if he pushes in the cigar lighter, the dome light comes on dimly. Using the wiring schmatic below, determine the cause.

☐ Task completed

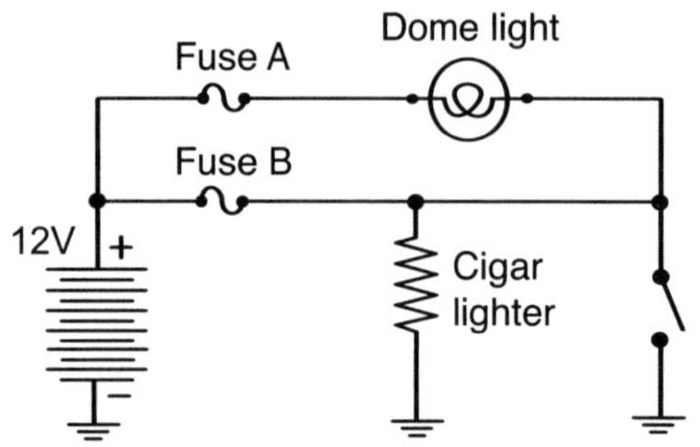

Problems Encountered

____

____

____

Instructor's Comments

____

____

____

☐ JOB SHEET / AT 103-26

Inspect and Test a Headlight Switch

Name ______________________________ Station ________________ Date ________________

Objective

Upon completion of this job sheet, you will have demonstrated the ability to check the operation of a headlight switch with an ohmmeter. You must be able to perform these task(s) in order to pass the **ASE** test for: **Electrical Systems.** Before beginning to do this Job Sheet, refer to **Chapter 20** in the AUTOMOTIVE TECHNOLOGY book for additional information.

Tools and Materials:

AUTOMOTIVE TECHNOLOGY 4e (Delmar Cengage Learning)

A vehicle

A wiring diagram for the vehicle

A DMM

Protective Gear:

Goggles or safety glasses with side shields

NATEF TASKS
VI. Electrical/Electronic Systems
Category: A
Task: 7 (P-2)
Task: 8 (P-1)
Task: 9 (P-1)
Task: 10 (P-1)
Category: E
Task: 1 (P-1)

Describe the vehicle being worked on:

Year __________ Make ________________________ Model ________________________

VIN ________________________ Engine type and size ________________________

PROCEDURE

1. Put the headlight switch in all possible positions and observe what lights are controlled by each position. List each position and the controlled lights below.

    ____

    ____

    ____

    ____

    ____

    ____

    ____

    ____

2. Locate the headlight switch in the wiring diagram and draw the switch with each possible connection and possible position. Label the lights controlled by each position of the switch.

3. Remove the fuse to the headlights or disconnect the battery's negative cable.

    Remove the headlight switch by following the procedures outlined in the service manual. Describe the procedure to your instructor before removing the headlight.

    Instructor's okay to move to the next step ______.

4. Identify the various terminals of the switch and list the particular terminals that should have continuity in the various switch positions.

5. Connect the ohmmeter across these terminals, one switch position at a time, and record your readings below:

6. Based on the above test, what are your conclusions about the switch?

7. Reinstall the switch and connect the negative battery cable or reinstall the fuse. Then check the operation of the headlights.

Problems Encountered

Instructor's Comments

☐ JOB SHEET / AT 103-27

Turn Signal Malfunction (Fault #1)

Name ______________________ Station ______________ Date ______________

Objective

Upon completion of this job sheet, you will demonstrate the ability to diagnose a common electrical system fault using a DVOM, an electrical schematic, and diagnostic charts.

NATEF TASKS
VI. Electrical/Electronic Systems
Category: E
Task: 3 (P-2)

Tools and Materials:

AUTOMOTIVE TECHNOLOGY 4e (Delmar Cengage Learning)

Instructor Notes

All-Data®

DVOM

Turn Signal Diagnostic Chart

Light Board Model #205

Light/Blower/Fuel System electrical diagnostic schematic

Protective Gear:

Safety glasses

Describe the vehicle being worked on:

Year __________ Make ______________________ Model ______________________

VIN ______________________ Engine type and size ______________________

PROCEDURE

A customer indicates that the turn signals and hazard lights are inoperative on her vehicle.

1. Utilizing the Light/Blower/Fuel System electrical diagnostic schematic and starting from the "power in" terminal, list the circuit components of the turn signal system **in sequence,** ending at the turn signal lights.

   a. ____

   b. ____

   c. ____

   d. ____

   e. ____

2. Utilizing to your diagnostic chart and the description of the problem, determine the appropriate diagnostic path to follow. Actuate the switch when necessary.

   a. What is the first component of the circuit you will check? ______________________

   b. Is there power at the component? ______________ Voltage? ______________

3. If there were no power at the fuse, what "up-stream" components would you check?

   a. ________________________________

   b. ________________________________

   c. ________________________________

4. Using your DVOM or test-light:

   a. Test power to the flasher. Is there power? ________________________

   b. Test power to the Turn Signal Switch. Is there power? ____________

   c. Test the ground at the Turn Signal Switch. Is there ground? ________

   What two possible circuit malfunctions does this indicate to you to this point?

   ____

   ____

5. Using your DVOM, how can the two possibilities be checked to isolate and identify the problem?

   ____

   ____

Problems Encountered

____

____

____

Instructor's Comments

____

____

____

☐ JOB SHEET / AT 103-28

Turn Signal Malfunction (Fault #2)

Name ______________________________ Station ________________ Date ________________

Objective

Upon completion of this job sheet, you will demonstrate the ability to diagnose a common electrical system fault using a DVOM, an electrical schematic, and diagnostic charts.

NATEF TASKS
VI. Electrical/Electronic Systems
Category: E
Task: 3 (P-2)

Tools and Materials:

AUTOMOTIVE TECHNOLOGY 4e (Delmar Cengage Learning)
Instructor notes
All-Data®
DVOM
Turn Signal Diagnostic Chart
Light Board Model #205
Light/Blower/Fuel System electrical diagnostic schematic

Protective Gear:

Safety glasses

Describe the vehicle being worked on:

Year __________ Make ________________________ Model ________________________

VIN ________________________ Engine type and size ________________________

PROCEDURE

A customer indicates that the left front turn signal is inoperative on her vehicle.

1. Utilizing the Light/Blower/Fuel System electrical diagnostic schematic and starting from the "power in" terminal, list the circuit components of the turn signal system **in sequence,** ending at the turn signal lights.

   a. ____

   b. ____

   c. ____

   d. ____

   e. ____

2. Utilizing to your diagnostic chart and the description of the problem, determine the appropriate diagnostic path to follow, actuating the switch when necessary.

   a. What is the first component it indicates to check? ________________

   b. Is there voltage going to the component? ________________

c. What is the voltage after the component? ____________________

What does this indicate? ______________________________

3. If the component is good, what is the next malfunction indicated on the chart to check?

____

4. Using your DVOM, test for a faulty ground at the malfunctioning turn signal light>

a. Is there a functioning ground connection? ____________________

b. How did you confirm your findings?

____

____

Problems Encountered

____

____

____

Instructor's Comments

____

____

____

☐ JOB SHEET / AT 103-29

Parking (Marker) Light Malfunction (Fault #3)

Name ____________________ Station ______________ Date ______________

Objective

Upon completion of this job sheet, you will demonstrate the ability to diagnose a common electrical system fault using a DVOM, an electrical schematic, and diagnostic charts.

NATEF TASKS
VI. Electrical/Electronic Systems
Category: E
Task: 1 (P-1)
Task: 3 (P-2)

Tools and Materials:

AUTOMOTIVE TECHNOLOGY 4e (Delmar Cengage Learning)
Instructor Notes
All-Data®
DVOM
Light Board Model #205
Light/Blower/Fuel System electrical diagnostic schematic

Protective Gear:

Safety glasses

Describe the vehicle being worked on:

Year ________ Make ____________________ Model ____________________

VIN ____________________ Engine type and size ____________________

PROCEDURE

A customer indicates that the front parking lights are inoperative on her vehicle.

1. Utilizing the Light/Blower/Fuel System electrical diagnostic schematic and starting from the "power in" terminal, list the circuit components of the parking (marker) lights **in sequence,** ending at the marker lights.

   a. ____

   b. ____

   c. ____

   d. ____

2. Using the Light/Blower/Fuel System electrical diagnostic schematic, what other lights are also parts of the marker light circuit?

   ____

   ____

   ____

3. Actuating the headlight switch, test the voltage at the tail lights.

   Voltage? ____________ v.

4. Test for power at **both** front parking (marker) lights. Is there power? ___________

   Voltage? ___________

5. Test for voltage **across** both marker lights. Is there power? ___________

   Voltage? ___________

6. Using your DVOM, test for ground connection at the marker lights.

   a. Is a ground connection indicated? ___________

   b. If a faulty ground connection exists, use your DVOM to confirm your diagnosis. How did you confirm your findings?

   ____

Problems Encountered

____

____

____

Instructor's Comments

____

____

____

☐ JOB SHEET / AT 103-30

Turn Signal Malfunction (Fault #4)

Name ______________________ Station ______________ Date ______________

Objective

Upon completion of this job sheet, you will demonstrate the ability to diagnose a common electrical system fault using a DVOM, an electrical schematic, and diagnostic charts.

NATEF TASKS
VI. Electrical/Electronic Systems
Category: E
Task: 3 (P-2)

Tools and Materials:

AUTOMOTIVE TECHNOLOGY 4e (Delmar Cengage Learning)
Instructor Notes
All-Data®
DVOM
Turn Signal Diagnostic Chart
Light Board Model #205
Light/Blower/Fuel System electrical diagnostic schematic

Protective Gear:

Safety glasses

Describe the vehicle being worked on:

Year ________ Make ____________________ Model ____________________

VIN ____________________ Engine type and size ____________________

PROCEDURE

A customer indicates that the right front turn signal light is dim on her vehicle.

1. Utilizing the Light/Blower/Fuel System electrical diagnostic schematic and starting from the "power in" terminal, list the circuit components of the turn signal system **in sequence,** ending at the turn signal lights.

   a. ____

   b. ____

   c. ____

   d. ____

2. Utilizing your diagnostic chart and the description of the problem, determine the appropriate diagnostic path to follow.

   What malfunction is indicated as probable? ____________________

3. Test for voltage at the fuse block Fuse # ____________Voltage ? ____________ v.

4. At the turn signal switch, what are the two terminal numbers for the front turn signal lamps, and what are the peak voltage readings when actuated?

   Terminal # ______________ Voltage ______________

   Terminal # ______________ Voltage ______________

5. Take voltage peak (pulse) readings at the two front turn signal lamps?

   Left turn signal voltage ______________

   Right turn signal voltage ______________

6. What does this indicate? ____

   ____

Problems Encountered

____

____

____

Instructor's Comments

____

____

____

☐ JOB SHEET / AT 103-31

Brake Light Malfunction (Fault #5)

Name ______________________ Station ______________ Date ______________

Objective

Upon completion of this job sheet, you will demonstrate the ability to diagnose a common electrical system fault using a DVOM, an electrical schematic, and diagnostic charts.

NATEF TASKS
VI. Electrical/Electronic Systems
Category: E
Task: 3 (P-2)

Tools and Materials:

AUTOMOTIVE TECHNOLOGY 4e (Delmar Cengage Learning)
Instructor Notes
All-Data®
DVOM
Turn Signal Diagnostic Chart
Light Board Model #205
Light/Blower/Fuel System electrical diagnostic schematic

Protective Gear:

Safety glasses

Describe the vehicle being worked on:

Year ________ Make ____________________ Model ____________________

VIN ____________________ Engine type and size ____________________

PROCEDURE

A customer indicates that the brake lights are dim on her vehicle.

1. Utilizing the Light/Blower/Fuel System electrical diagnostic schematic and starting from the "power in" terminal, list the circuit components of the brake light system **in sequence,** ending at the brake lights.

   a. ____

   b. ____

   c. ____

   d. ____

   e. ____

2. Test for voltage out of the fuse block (brake light fuse).

   Fuse # ____________ Voltage # ____________ v.

3. What function does the turn signal switch serve in the brake light circuit?

____

4. Continuing to the next component in the system, test for voltage at the brake light switch. Voltage?

____

5. Actuate the brake light switch and test voltage.

What should the voltage be? _______________ What is the voltage drop? _______________

6. What does this indicate? ____

Problems Encountered

____

____

____

Instructor's Comments

____

____

____

☐ JOB SHEET / AT 103-32

Taillight/Brake Light Malfunction (Fault #6)

Name ______________________________ Station __________________ Date __________________

Objective

Upon completion of this job sheet, you will demonstrate the ability to diagnose a common electrical system fault using a DVOM, an electrical schematic, and diagnostic charts.

NATEF TASKS
VI. Electrical/Electronic Systems
Category: E
Task: 1 (P-1)

Tools and Materials:

AUTOMOTIVE TECHNOLOGY 4e (Delmar Cengage Learning)
Instructor notes
All-Data®
DVOM
Turn Signal Diagnostic Chart
Light Board Model #205
Light/Blower/Fuel System electrical diagnostic schematic

Protective Gear:

Safety glasses

Describe the vehicle being worked on:

Year __________ Make __________________________ Model __________________________

VIN __________________________ Engine type and size __________________________

PROCEDURE

A customer indicates that the right side taillight and right side brake light are dim.

1. What is the common malfunction occurring in both lamps?

 ____

2. Utilizing the Light/Blower/Fuel System electrical diagnostic schematic, what common components of the circuit are shared by the two lamps?

 ____

 ____

 ____

3. According to your Turn Signal Diagnostic Chart, what type of malfunction would cause the symptom exhibited?

 ____

4. Of the shared circuit components identified earlier, which one would cause the malfunction indicated?

____

5. Utilizing your DVOM and the chassis ground terminal, what is the voltage at the actuated:

Left Tail Light ______________ Right Tail Light ______________

Left Barke Light ____________ Right Brake Light ____________

What should they be? __________________________

6. Utilizing your DVOM and the **left** tail brake light assembly ground connection terminal, what is the voltage at the:

Left Tail Light ________________

Left Brake Light _______________

What should it be? _____________

7. Utilizing your DVOM and the **right** tail brake light assembly ground connection terminal, what is the voltage at the:

Right Tail Light ________________

Right Brake Light _______________

What should it be? _____________

8. What does this indicate? ____

Problems Encountered

____

____

____

Instructor's Comments

____

____

____

☐ JOB SHEET / AT 103-33

Back-up Light Malfunction (Fault #8)

Name ______________________ Station ______________ Date ______________

Objective

Upon completion of this job sheet, you will demonstrate the ability to diagnose a common electrical system fault using a DVOM, an electrical schematic, and diagnostic charts.

NATEF TASKS
VI. Electrical/Electronic Systems
Category: E
Task: 1 (P-1)

Tools and Materials:

AUTOMOTIVE TECHNOLOGY 4e (Delmar Cengage Learning)
Instructor notes
All-Data®
DVOM
Turn Signal Diagnostic Chart
Light Board Model #205
Light/Blower/Fuel System electrical diagnostic schematic

Protective Gear:

Safety glasses

Describe the vehicle being worked on:

Year __________ Make ____________________ Model ____________________

VIN ____________________ Engine type and size ____________________

PROCEDURE

A customer indicates that the left back-up light is inoperative.

1. Utilizing the Light/Blower/Fuel System electrical diagnostic schematic and starting from the "power in" terminal, list the circuit components of the back-up lights **in sequence**, ending at the back-up lights.

   a. ____

   b. ____

   c. ____

   d. ____

2. Using the chassis ground terminal as your ground source, record voltage readings at the following circuit locations with the back-up light switch closed:

   a. Fuse # ________ ____________ v.

   b. Back-up light switch ____________ v.

c. Left back-up light ____________ v. Right back-up light ______________ v.

d. **Across** the left lamp ______________ v. **Across** the right lamp _____________ v.

3. Using the ground terminal of the **right** back-up light as your ground connection, what is the voltage across the right lamp? ______________ v.
4. Using the ground terminal of the **left** back-up light as your ground connection, what is the voltage across the left lamp? ______________ v.
5. What does this indicate? ____

Problems Encountered

____

____

____

Instructor's Comments

____

____

____

☐ JOB SHEET / AT 103-34

Headlight Malfunction (Fault #9)

Name ______________________ Station ______________ Date ______________

Objective

Upon completion of this job sheet, you will demonstrate the ability to diagnose a common electrical system fault using a DVOM, an electrical schematic, and diagnostic charts.

NATEF TASKS
VI. Electrical/Electronic Systems
Category: E
Task: 2 (P-2)

Tools and Materials:

AUTOMOTIVE TECHNOLOGY 4e (Delmar Cengage Learning)
Instructor Notes
All-Data®
DVOM
Turn Signal Diagnostic Chart
Light Board Model #205
Light/Blower/Fuel System electrical diagnostic schematic

Protective Gear:

Safety glasses

Describe the vehicle being worked on:

Year ________ Make ____________________ Model ____________________

VIN ____________________ Engine type and size ____________________

PROCEDURE

A customer indicates that low beam headlights are inoperative.

1. Utilizing the Light/Blower/Fuel System electrical diagnostic schematic and starting from the "power in" terminal, list the circuit components of the headlight system **in sequence,** ending at the headlights.

   a. ____

   b. ____

   c. ____

   d. ____

   e. ____

   f. ____

2. Using the chassis ground terminal as your ground source and with the headlight switch turned on, record voltage readings at the following circuit locations and components with the headlight switch and high-beams on:

   a. Fuse # _______________ Voltage ? _______________ v.

   b. Headlight Switch (Power) _______________ v. Switch (Headlight) _______________ v.

   c. High Beam Relay: Power Terminal # _______________ Voltage _______________ v.

   d. Low Beam Relay: Power Terminal # _______________ Voltage _______________ v.

   e. High Beam Relay: Output Terminal # _______________ Voltage _______________ v.

   f. Low Beam Relay: Output Terminal # _______________ Voltage _______________ v.

3. What does this indicate to this point? ____

4. Using the DVOM, test the integrity of the relay ground connection.

   a. Using the low beam relay ground connection, what is the voltage across Low Beam Relay (Power Terminal)? _______________ v.

   b. Where is the ground source for the high beam relay? ______________________________

5. What are your conclusions? ____

____

Problems Encountered

____

____

____

Instructor's Comments

____

____

____

☐ JOB SHEET / AT 103-35

Headlight Malfunction (Fault #10)

Name ______________________________ Station __________________ Date __________________

Objective

Upon completion of this job sheet, you will demonstrate the ability to diagnose a common electrical system fault using a DVOM, an electrical schematic, and diagnostic charts.

NATEF TASKS
VI. Electrical/Electronic Systems
Category: E
Task: 2 (P-2)

Tools and Materials:

AUTOMOTIVE TECHNOLOGY 4e (Delmar Cengage Learning)
Instructor notes
All-Data®
DVOM
Turn Signal Diagnostic Chart
Light Board Model #205
Light/Blower/Fuel System electrical diagnostic schematic

Protective Gear:

Safety glasses

Describe the vehicle being worked on:

Year __________ Make __________________________ Model __________________________

VIN __________________________ Engine type and size __________________________

PROCEDURE

A customer indicates that high beam headlights are inoperative.

1. Utilizing the Light/Blower/Fuel System electrical diagnostic schematic and starting from the "power in" terminal, list the circuit components of the headlight system **in sequence,** ending at the headlights.

   a. ____

   b. ____

   c. ____

   d. ____

   e. ____

   f. ____

2. Using the chassis ground terminal as your ground source, record voltage readings at the following circuit locations with the headlight switch on:

   a. Fuse # __________ ______________ v.

   b. Headlight Switch (Input-B) ______________ v. Output-H ______________ v..

   c. High Beam Relay: Power Terminal # ______________ Voltage ______________ v.

   d. Low Beam Relay: Power Terminal # ______________ Voltage ______________ v.

3. What does this indicate? ____

Problems Encountered

____

____

____

Instructor's Comments

____

____

____

☐ JOB SHEET / AT 103-37

Low Fuel Warning Lamp Malfunction (Fault #12)

Name ______________________________ Station __________________ Date __________________

Objective

Upon completion of this job sheet, you will demonstrate the ability to diagnose a common electrical system fault using a DVOM, an electrical schematic, and diagnostic charts.

NATEF TASKS
VI. Electrical/Electronic Systems
Category: F
Task: 1 (P-3)

Tools and Materials:

AUTOMOTIVE TECHNOLOGY 4e (Delmar Cengage Learning)
Instructor notes
All-Data®
DVOM
Turn Signal Diagnostic Chart
Light Board Model #205
Light/Blower/Fuel System electrical diagnostic schematic

Protective Gear:

Safety glasses

Describe the vehicle being worked on:

Year __________ Make __________________________ Model __________________________

VIN __________________________ Engine type and size __________________________

PROCEDURE

A customer indicates that the low fuel warning lamp is illuminated at all times.

1. Utilizing the Light/Blower/Fuel System electrical diagnostic schematic and starting from the "power in" terminal, list the circuit components of the fuel warning system **in sequence,** ending at the warning light.

   a. ____

   b. ____

   c. ____

   d. ____

   e. ____

   f. ____

2. Using the chassis ground terminal as your ground source, record voltage readings at the following circuit locations:

   a. Fuse # __________ ______________ v.

   b. Fuel Level Sensor—Input Term. __________ v. Output Term. __________ v.

Normal Baseline Observation:

3. With Fault #12 **disengaged,** test and observe the normal voltage signal at the **Fuel Level Sensor** by probing its signal terminal and rotating the fuel sensor knob.

   What is the range of voltage from the "Full" mark to the "Empty" mark of the fuel gauge?

   Full __________ v. Empty __________ v.

4. Starting at the "Full" mark, slowly rotate the sensor knob counterclockwise to empty the tank while observing the voltage drop at the **Fuel Level Sensor.**

   a. At what voltage reading is the low fuel warning light actuated? __________ v.

   b. With the warning light "on," what is the voltage at the **Warning Light Sensor**?

5. Probe the **Low Fuel Warning** light sensor while turning the **Fuel Level Sensor** knob counterclockwise in the same manner as before.

   a. What is the range of voltage from the "Full" mark to the "Empty" mark of the fuel gauge?

      Fuel __________ v. Empty __________ v.

   b. At what voltage does the **Warning Light Sensor** actuate the **Low Fuel Warning Light?**

      Actuating Voltage __________ v.

6. What effect does the Fuel Level Sensor have on the operation of the Low Fuel Sensor?

   ____

   ____

Malfunction

7. Actuate Fault #12 and repeat the same probes and observations of the two sensor as before.

   a. At the **Fuel Level Sensor,** what is the range of voltage from the "Full" mark to the "Empty" mark of the fuel gauge?

      Full __________ v. Empty __________ v.

   b. Has the malfunction (fault) had any effect on the **Fuel Level Sensor?** ______________

   c. At the **Fuel Level Sensor,** what is the range of voltage from the "Full" mark to the "Empty" mark of the fuel gauge?

      Full __________ v. Empty __________ v.

   d. Has the malfunction (fault) had any effect on the **Low Fuel Warning Light Sensor?** __________

8. What does this indicate in regard to the malfunction (fault)? ______________________________

   ____

Problems Encountered

____

____

____

Instructor's Comments

____

____

____

☐ JOB SHEET / AT 103-39

Low Fuel Warning Lamp Malfunction (Fault #14)

Name ______________________ Station ______________ Date ______________

Objective

Upon completion of this job sheet, you will demonstrate the ability to diagnose a common electrical system fault using a DVOM, an electrical schematic, and diagnostic charts.

NATEF TASKS
VI. Electrical/Electronic Systems
Category: F
Task: 1 (P-1)
Task: 2 (P-3)
Task: 3 (P-1)
Task: 4 (P-2)

Tools and Materials:

AUTOMOTIVE TECHNOLOGY (Delmar)
Instructor notes
All-Data®
DVOM
Turn Signal Diagnostic Chart
Light Board Model #205
Light/Blower/Fuel System electrical diagnostic schematic

Protective Gear:

Safety glasses

Describe the vehicle being worked on:

Year ________ Make ____________________ Model ____________________

VIN ____________________ Engine type and size ____________________

PROCEDURE

A customer indicates that the low fuel-warning lamp is dim.

1. Utilizing the Light/Blower/Fuel System electrical diagnostic schematic and starting from the "power in" terminal, list the circuit components of the fuel warning system **in sequence,** ending at the warning light.

   a. ____

   b. ____

   c. ____

   d. ____

   e. ____

   f. ____

2. Using the Turn Signal Diagnostic Chart, what condition is usually the cause of a dim lamp?

____

3. Actuate the Low Fuel Warning Light. Testing at the warning lamp ("+" side), what is the voltage drop using the "Chassis Ground?" _______________ v.

4. What is the voltage drop across the warning lamp ("+") to the lamp ground connection? _______________ v.

5. What does this indicate? _______________

____

Problems Encountered

____

____

____

Instructor's Comments

____

____

____

☐ JOB SHEET / AT 103-40

Blower Motor Malfunction (Fault #15)

Name ______________________ Station ______________ Date ______________

Objective

Upon completion of this job sheet, you will demonstrate the ability to diagnose a common electrical system fault using a DVOM, an electrical schematic, and diagnostic charts.

NATEF TASKS
VI. Electrical/Electronic Systems
Category: A
Task: 1 (P-1)
Task: 2 (P-1)
Task: 3 (P-1)
Category: H
Task: 1 (P-2)

Tools and Materials:

AUTOMOTIVE TECHNOLOGY 4e (Delmar Cengage Learning)
Instructor notes
All-Data®
DVOM
Turn Signal Diagnostic Chart
Light Board Model #205
Light/Blower/Fuel System electrical diagnostic schematic

Protective Gear:

Safety glasses

Describe the vehicle being worked on:

Year ________ Make ____________________ Model ____________________

VIN ____________________ Engine type and size ____________________

PROCEDURE

A customer indicates that the blower motor is inoperative.

1. Utilizing the Light/Blower/Fuel System electrical diagnostic schematic and starting from the "power in" terminal, list the circuit components of the blower motor system **in sequence,** ending at the blower motor.

   a. ____

   b. ____

   c. ____

   d. ____

2. Using the chassis ground terminal as your ground source, record voltage readings at the following circuit locations while operating the blower motor switch:

   a. Fuse # ________ ____________ v.

   b. Blower Motor Switch Power Terminal (High) ____________ v.

c. Blower Motor Switch Output Terminals

Low _______________ v. Medium _______________ v.

d. Test for voltage between the fuse and the Blower Motor Switch Output Terminals?

Low _______________ v. Medium _______________ v.

3. What malfunction does this indicate? ____

____

Problems Encountered

____

____

____

Instructor's Comments

____

____

____

☐ JOB SHEET / AT 103-41

Blower Motor Malfunction (Fault #16)

Name ______________________ Station ______________ Date ______________

Objective

Upon completion of this job sheet, you will demonstrate the ability to diagnose a common electrical system fault using a DVOM, an electrical schematic, and diagnostic charts.

NATEF TASKS
VI. Electrical/Electronic Systems
Category: A
Task: 1 (P-1)
Task: 2 (P-1)
Task: 3 (P-1)
Category: H
Task: (P-2)

Tools and Materials:

AUTOMOTIVE TECHNOLOGY 4e (Delmar Cengage Learning)
Instructor notes
All-Data®
DVOM
Turn Signal Diagnostic Chart
Light Board Model #205
Light/Blower/Fuel System electrical diagnostic schematic

Protective Gear:

Safety glasses

Describe the vehicle being worked on:

Year __________ Make ______________________ Model ______________________

VIN ______________________ Engine type and size ______________________

PROCEDURE

A customer indicates that the blower motor operates on high speed only.

1. Utilizing the Light/Blower/Fuel System electrical diagnostic schematic and starting from the "power in" terminal, list the circuit components of the blower motor system **in sequence,** ending at the blower motor.

   a. ____

   b. ____

   c. ____

   d. ____

2. Using the chassis ground terminal as your ground source, record voltage readings at the following circuit locations while operating the blower motor switch:

   a. Fuse # __________ ______________ v.

   b. Blower Motor Power Switch Power Terminal (High) ____________ v.

   What does this indicate? ____

   ____

c. Blower Motor Switch Output Terminals

Low _______________ v. Medium _______________ v.

d. What is the voltage drop between the fuse and the Blower Motor Switch Terminals?

Low _______________ v. Medium _______________ v.

3. What does this indicate? ____

____

Problems Encountered

____

____

____

Instructor's Comments

____

____

____

☐ JOB SHEET / AT 103-42

Blower Motor Malfunction (Fault #17)

Name ______________________________ Station __________________ Date __________________

Objective

Upon completion of this job sheet, you will demonstrate the ability to diagnose a common electrical system fault using a DVOM, an electrical schematic, and diagnostic charts.

Tools and Materials:

AUTOMOTIVE TECHNOLOGY 4e (Delmar Cengage Learning)
Instructor notes
All-Data®
DVOM
Turn Signal Diagnostic Chart
Light Board Model #205
Light/Blower/Fuel System electrical diagnostic schematic

NATEF TASKS
VI. Electrical/Electronic Systems
Category: A
Task: 1 (P-1)
Task: 2 (P-2)
Task: 3 (P-1)
Category: H
Task: (p-2)

Protective Gear:

Safety glasses

Describe the vehicle being worked on:

Year __________ Make __________________________ Model __________________________

VIN __________________________ Engine type and size __________________________

PROCEDURE

A customer indicates that the blower motor operates very slowly and may not operate at all on the low speed setting.

1. Utilizing the Light/Blower/Fuel System electrical diagnostic schematic and starting from the "power in" terminal, list the circuit components of the blower motor system **in sequence,** ending at the blower motor.

   a. ____

   b. ____

   c. ____

   d. ____

2. Using the chassis ground terminal as your ground source, record voltage readings at the following circuit locations while operating the blower motor switch:

   a. Fuse # __________ _______________ v.

   b. Blower Motor Switch Power Terminal (High) _______________ v.

c. Blower Motor Switch Output Terminals

Low ______________ v. Medium ______________ v.

3. While operating the Blower Motor Switch, what is the voltage drop between the fuse and the respective Output Terminals?

Low ______________ v. Medium ______________ v. High ______________ v.

4. What does this indicate? ____

____

Problems Encountered

____

____

____

Instructor's Comments

____

____

____

☐ JOB SHEET / AT 103-43

Fuel Pump Malfunction (Fault #18)

Name ______________________________ Station __________________ Date __________________

Objective

Upon completion of this job sheet, you will demonstrate the ability to diagnose a common electrical system fault using a DVOM, an electrical schematic, and diagnostic charts.

Tools and Materials:

AUTOMOTIVE TECHNOLOGY 4e (Delmar Cengage Learning)

Instructor notes

All-Data®

DVOM

Turn Signal Diagnostic Chart

Light Board Model #205

Light/Blower/Fuel System electrical diagnostic schematic

NATEF TASKS
VI. Electrical/Electronic Systems
Category: A
Task: 1 (P-1)
Task: 2 (P-1)
Task: 3 (P-1)
Task: 11 (P-2)
Task: 15 (P-1)

Protective Gear:

Safety glasses

Describe the vehicle being worked on:

Year __________ Make __________________________ Model __________________________

VIN __________________________ Engine type and size __________________________

PROCEDURE

A customer complains of a no start condition. Upon initial diagnostic check, you determine that the fuel pump is inoperative.

1. Utilizing the Light/Blower/Fuel System electrical diagnostic schematic and starting from the "power in" terminal, list the circuit components of the fuel pump system **in sequence,** ending at the fuel pump.

   a. ____

   b. ____

   c. ____

   d. ____

   e. ____

2. Using the chassis ground terminal as your ground source, record voltage readings at the following circuit locations with the fuel pump switch actuated:

   a. Fuse # __________ ______________ v.

   b. Fuel Pump Relay Terminals

   Power (30) ______ v. Applied Power (86) ______ v. Fuel Pump Power (87) ______ v.

3. What does this indicate? ______________________________

____

4. What terminal # is the relay ground connection? ______________________________

5. Using the **Fuel Pump Relay** ground source, test the relay power terminals again.

6. What is the result? ______________________________

7. What does this indicate? ______________________________

Problems Encountered

____

____

____

Instructor's Comments

____

____

____

☐ JOB SHEET / AT 103-44

Fuel Pump Malfunction (Fault #19)

Name ______________________________ Station __________________ Date __________________

Objective

Upon completion of this job sheet, you will demonstrate the ability to diagnose a common electrical system fault using a DVOM, an electrical schematic, and diagnostic charts.

NATEF TASKS
VI. Electrical/Electronic Systems
Category: A
Task: 1 (P-1)
Task: 2 (P-1)
Task: 3 (P-1)
Task: 11 (P-2)
Task: 15 (P-1)

Tools and Materials:

AUTOMOTIVE TECHNOLOGY 4e (Delmar Cengage Learning)
Instructor notes
All-Data®
DVOM
Turn Signal Diagnostic Chart
Light Board Model #205
Light/Blower/Fuel System electrical diagnostic schematic

Protective Gear:

Safety glasses

Describe the vehicle being worked on:

Year ____________ Make ___________________________ Model ___________________________

VIN ___________________________ Engine type and size ___________________________

PROCEDURE

While diagnosing a customer complaint of a "buzzing" noise at all times, you find the fuel pump is running constantly.

1. Utilizing the Light/Blower/Fuel System electrical diagnostic schematic and starting from the "power in" terminal, list the circuit components of the fuel pump system **in sequence,** ending at the fuel pump.

   a. ____

   b. ____

   c. ____

   d. ____

   e. ____

2. Using the chassis ground terminal as your ground source, record voltage readings at the following circuit locations with the fuel pump switch both actuated and disengaged:

   a. Fuse # __________ _______________ v.

   b. Fuel Pump Switch "+" __________ v. Relay Side (Driver) __________ v.

c. Fuel Pump Relay Terminals (Switch Actuated)

Power (30) _________ v. Applied Power (86) _________ v. Fuel Pump Power (87) _________ v.

d. Fuel Pump Relay Terminals (Switch Disengaged)

Power (30) _________ v. Applied Power (86) _________ v. Fuel Pump Power (87) _________ v.

3. What does this indicate? ____

____

Problems Encountered

____

____

____

Instructor's Comments

____

____

____

☐ JOB SHEET / AT 103-45

Fuel Gauge Malfunction (Fault #20)

Name ______________________ Station ______________ Date ______________

Objective

Upon completion of this job sheet, you will demonstrate the ability to diagnose a common electrical system fault using a DVOM, an electrical schematic, and diagnostic charts.

NATEF TASKS
VI. Electrical/Electronic Systems
Category: F
Task: 1 (P-1)
Task: 2 (P-3)
Task: 3 (P-1)

Tools and Materials:

AUTOMOTIVE TECHNOLOGY 4e (Delmar Cengage Learning)
Instructor notes
All-Data®
DVOM
Turn Signal Diagnostic Chart
Light Board Model #205
Light/Blower/Fuel System electrical diagnostic schematic

Protective Gear:

Safety glasses

Describe the vehicle being worked on:

Year ________ Make ____________________ Model ____________________

VIN ____________________ Engine type and size ____________________

PROCEDURE

The customer indicates the fuel gauge is inoperative.

1. Utilizing the Light/Blower/Fuel System electrical diagnostic schematic and starting from the "power in" terminal, list the circuit components of the fuel gauge system **in sequence,** ending at the fuel gauge.

   a. ____

   b. ____

   c. ____

   d. ____

2. Using the chassis ground terminal as your ground source, record voltage readings at the following circuit locations:

   a. Fuse # ________ ____________ v.

   b. Is there power to the Fuel Level Sensor? ________ ________ v.

   c. Is there power to the Low Fuel Sensor? ________ ________ v.

d. While turning the fuel sensor dial (variable resistor) from the "Full" mark to the "Empty" mark, what are the voltage "output" readings of the Fuel Level Sensor?

From ________ v. to ________ v.

3. What effect to voltage would you expect from a variable resistor?

____

____

4. What malfunction does the absence of this effect indicate?

____

____

Problems Encountered

____

____

____

Instructor's Comments

____

____

____

☐ JOB SHEET / AT 103-47

Adjust or Replace Stop-light Switch

Name ______________________ Station ______________ Date ______________

Objective

Upon completion of this job sheet, you will have demonstrated the ability to test and replace a stop-light switch. You must be able to perform these task(s) in order to pass the **ASE** test for: **Electrical and Brake Systems.** Before beginning to do this Job Sheet, refer to **Chapter 20** in the AUTOMOTIVE TECHNOLOGY book for additional information.

NATEF TASKS
VI. Electrical/Electronic Systems
Category: E
Task: 1 (P-1)
Task: 2 (P-2)
Task: 3 (P-2)

Tools and Materials:

AUTOMOTIVE TECHNOLOGY 4e (Delmar Cengage Learning)
12-volt test light
Appropriate screwdrivers
Jumper wire
Service manual

Protective Gear:

Goggles or safety glasses with side shields

Describe the vehicle being worked on:

Year ________ Make ____________________ Model ____________________

VIN ____________________ Engine type and size ____________________

PROCEDURE

1. At the stop-light switch, connect the two stop-light wires together with a jumper wire. Brake lights should light. When a defective wire or switch is located, repair as instructed in service manual. ☐ Task completed

2. If the stop-light switch is defective, disconnect the wire harness connector from the switch. Remove the retainer, slide stop-light switch and pushrod, and remove the washer and then the switch by sliding switch up or down (Figure 11). ☐ Task completed

3. Position the switch so U-shaped side is nearest the pedal and directly over or under the pin. Then slide the switch up and down, trapping the master cylinder pushrod and bushing between the switch side plates. ☐ Task completed

4. Push the switch and pushrod assembly firmly toward the brake pedal arm. Assemble the outside washer to the pin and install the retainer to hold the entire assembly. ☐ Task completed

5. Attach the connector to the switch. If the switch needs adjusting, adjust the switch in the mounting clips or with the nuts that hold the switch in the mounting bracket. Adjust, as necessary, to allow the switch's plunger to extend enough to make electrical contact when the pedal is depressed. ☐ Task completed

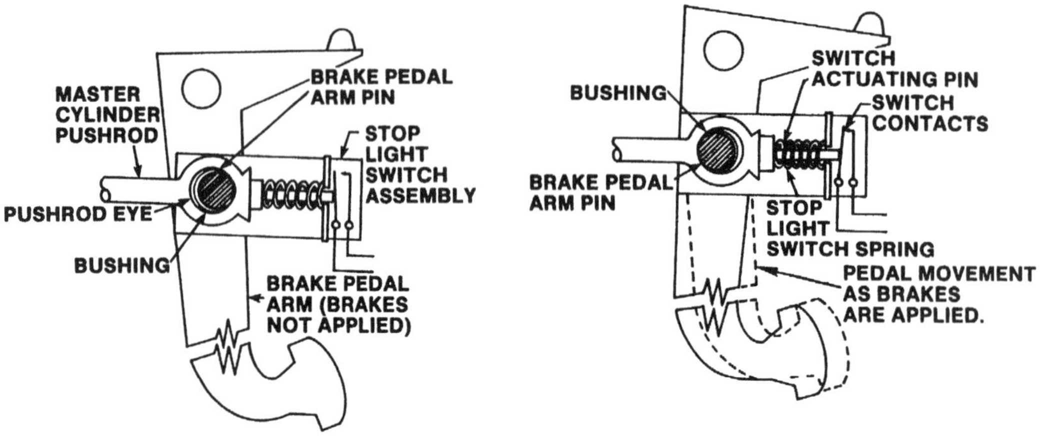

Figure 11. Stop-light switch.

6. Test the operation of the stop lights. ☐ Task completed

Problems Encountered

____

____

____

Instructor's Comments

____

____

____

CASE STUDY

A customer brings in her vehicle and complains that the right headlight is quite a bit dimmer than the left headlight. Outline the steps that should be taken to identify the exact cause of the problem.

____

____

____

____

____

☐ JOB SHEET / AT 103-48

Headlight Aiming

Name ______________________ Station ______________ Date ______________

Objective

Upon completion of this job sheet, you will have demonstrated the ability to adjust the aim of headlights using portable headlight aiming equipment. You must be able to perform these task(s) in order to pass the **ASE** test for: **Electrical Systems.** Before beginning to do this Job Sheet, refer to **Chapter 20** in the AUTOMOTIVE TECHNOLOGY book for additional information.

Tools and Materials:

AUTOMOTIVE TECHNOLOGY 4e (Delmar Cengage Learning)

A vehicle with adjustable headlights

Portable headlight aiming kit

Hand tools

Protective Gear:

Goggles or safety glasses with side shields

Describe the vehicle being worked on:

Year ________ Make ____________________ Model ____________________

VIN ____________________ Engine type and size ____________________

PROCEDURE

1. Describe the type of headlights used on the vehicle.

   ____

   ____

2. Park the vehicle on a level floor.

   Install the calibrated aiming units to headlights. Make sure the adapters fit the headlight aiming pads on the lens. ☐ Task completed

3. Zero the horizontal adjustment dial. Are the split image target lines visible in the view port? ______________ If the lines cannot be seen, what should you do?

   ____

4. Turn the headlight horizontal adjusting screw until the split image target lines are aligned. Then repeat this for the other headlight. List any problems you may have had doing this.

   ____

   ____

5. Turn the vertical adjustment dial on the aiming unit to zero. ☐ Task completed

   Turn the vertical adjustment screw until the spirit level bubble is centered. ☐ Task completed

   Recheck your horizontal setting after adjusting the vertical. ☐ Task completed

6. List any problems you had making the vertical adjustment.

   ____

   ____

   ____

   ____

7. If the headlight assembly has four lamp assemblies, repeat steps 2 through 5 on the other two lamps. List below any problems you may have had doing this.

   ____

   ____

   ____

   ____

Problems Encountered

____

____

____

Instructor's Comments

____

____

____

REVIEW QUESTIONS

1. List three circuits that may be controlled by a typical multifunction switch:

____

____

____

2. What are the four basic types of headlights that are used in today's vehicles?

____

____

____

____

3. What causes most lamp failure? ______________________________

____

4. What is the purpose of the rheostat in the headlight switch? ______________________________

____

____

5. Technician A says some bulbs have a glass envelope that encloses the filament and if air enters the envelope, the oxygen would cause the filament to oxidize and burn up. Technician B says a standard sealed-beam headlamp does not surround the filament with its own glass envelope; instead, the inside of the lamp is typically filled with argon gas. Who is correct?

   a. Technician A
   b. Technician B
   c. Both A and B
   d. Neither A nor B

6. Technician A says it is normal to see some condensation on the inside of a composite headlight assembly. Technician B says skin oil on a halogen light bulb's glass envelope can shorten the life of the bulb. Who is correct?

   a. Technician A
   b. Technician B
   c. Both A and B
   d. Neither A nor B

7. True or false? The circuit for DRLs normally contains some kind of module that reduces the voltage applied to the headlights. ______________________________

8. How many wire connections are needed in a four-headlight system?

____

9. How many filaments are in each headlight in a two-headlight system?

____

10. Only one backup light works. Technician A says to check the backup light switch. Technician B says to check the bulb that is not burning. Who is correct?

    a. Technician A
    b. Technician B
    c. Both A and B
    d. Neither A nor B

ASE PREP TEST

1. Technician A says thermal plastics are the most common electrical insulators used today. Technician B says if the conductor size is doubled, the resistance for any given length is cut in half. Who is correct?

   a. Technician A
   b. Technician B
   c. Both A and B
   d. Neither A nor B

2. Technician A says one characteristic of a series circuit is that same current flows through all resistors. Technician B says the current through each leg will be different if the resistance values are different in a parallel circuit. Who is correct?

   a. Technician A
   b. Technician B
   c. Both A and B
   d. Neither A nor B

3. Technician A says a negative temperature coefficient thermistor is the most commonly used thermistor. Technician B says a commonly used reference voltage sensor is a switch. Who is correct?

   a. Technician A
   b. Technician B
   c. Both A and B
   d. Neither A nor B

4. Technician A says specifications given in service manuals are normally not RMS voltage readings. Technician B says RMS readings are not even close to being average meter readings. Who is correct?

   a. Technician A
   b. Technician B
   c. Both A and B
   d. Neither A nor B

5. Technician A says a parasitic drain test places the ammeter in series with the positive battery cable. Technician B says the maximum permissible current drain is 0.08 ampere. Who is correct?

   a. Technician A
   b. Technician B
   c. Both A and B
   d. Neither A nor B

6. Technician A says an open circuit voltage test reading of 12.0 volts or better indicates a fully charged battery. Technician B says a battery capacity test indicates how well a battery functions under load. Who is correct?

   a. Technician A
   b. Technician B
   c. Both A and B
   d. Neither A nor B

7. Technician A says the OBD II scan tool has freeze-frame capability. Technician B says trouble codes are set when the amperage signal is entirely out of its normal range. Who is correct?

   a. Technician A
   b. Technician B
   c. Both A and B
   d. Neither A nor B

8. Technician A says decoder circuits are a combination of OR gates used to provide a certain output. Technician B says a multiplexer is used to examine one of many outputes depending on a programmed priority rating. Who is correct?

   a. Technician A
   b. Technician B
   c. Both A and B
   d. Neither A nor B

9. Technician A says high voltage will cause lamps to burn out prematurely. Technician B says adaptive headlights respond in real time to the vehicle's current steering angle, yaw rate, and road speed. Who is correct?

   a. Technician A
   b. Technician B
   c. Both A and B
   d. Neither A nor B

10. Technician A says the accumulated mileage (kilometer) value of the digital display odometer is stored in a non-volatile memory. Technician B says if the speedometer has been replaced, there is no need to set the odometer reading of the new to match the old. Who is correct?
    a. Technician A
    b. Technician B
    c. Both A and B
    d. Neither A nor B
11. Technician A says the passive seat belt system is part of the inertia switch circuit. Technician B says it is important that both shoulder belts are replaced whenever either belt is stressed in a motor vehicle accident. Who is correct?
    a. Technician A
    b. Technician B
    c. Both A and B
    d. Neither A nor B
12. Technician A says the arming sensor must close before the air bag will deploy. Technician B says the yaw sensor must be tripped before the air bag will deploy. Who is correct?
    a. Technician A
    b. Technician B
    c. Both A and B
    d. Neither A nor B
13. In the charging system shown in Figure 12, the meter reading will show
    a. charging output voltages.
    b. indicator lamp operating voltage.
    c. charging circuit voltage drop.
    d. ignition switch voltage drop.

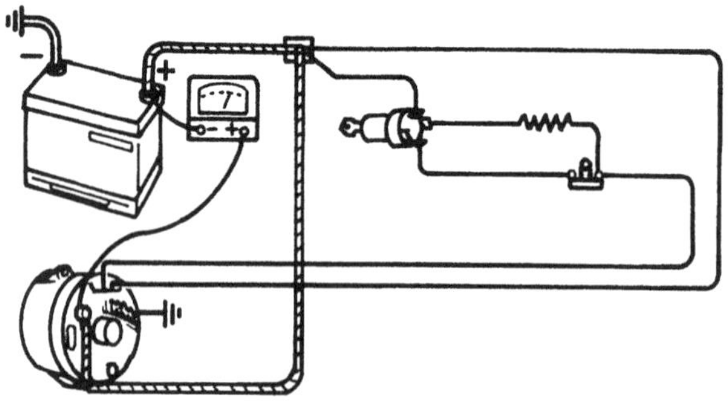

Figure 12. Charging system.

14. The oil pressure light stays on whenever the engine is running. The oil pressure has been checked and it meets specs. Technician A says that a ground in the circuit between the indicator light and the pressure switch could be the cause. Technician B says that an opening in the pressure switch could be the cause. Who is correct?
    a. Technician A
    b. Technician B
    c. Both A and B
    d. Neither A nor B
15. The ohmmeter needle does not move when connected as shown in Figure 13. This indicates that the rotor winding is
    a. shorted.
    b. grounded.
    c. complete.
    d. open.

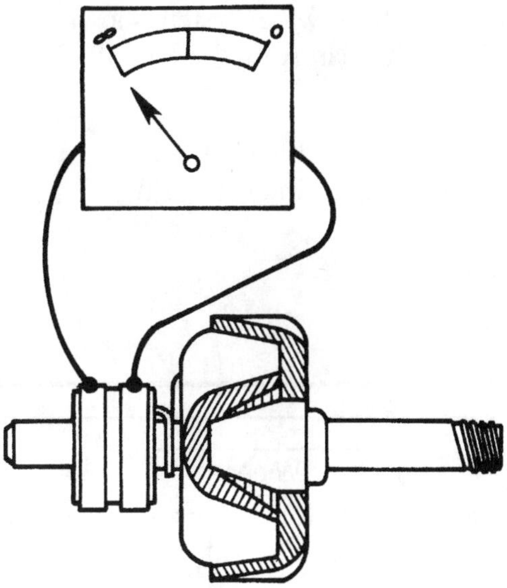

Figure 13. Ohmmeter connected across slip rings.

16. The light in the circuit shown in Figure 14 glows dimly. A technician connects a test light as shown. The test light burns at normal brightness. Technician A says that a bad ground at the light could be the cause. Technician B says that high resistance in the circuit from the battery to the light could be the cause. Who is correct?

    a. Technician A
    b. Technician B
    c. Both A and B
    d. Neither A nor B

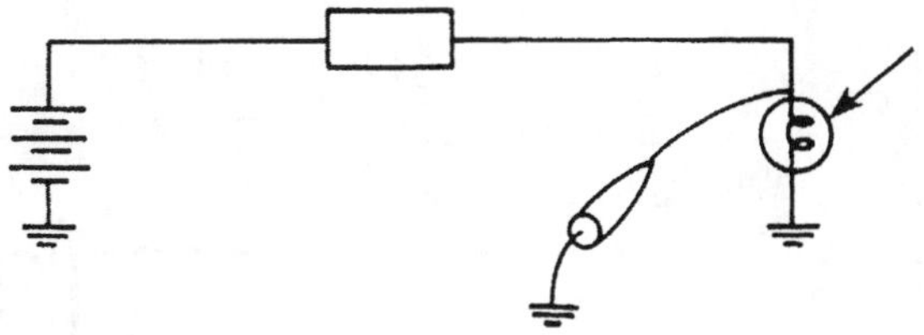

Figure 14. A test light connected to a simple circuit.

17. A voltmeter that is connected across the input and output terminals of an instrument cluster illumination lamp rheostat (dimmer control) indicates 12.6 volts with the switch in the maximum brightness position and the engine off. Which of the following statements is true?

    a. The voltage available at the lamps will be 12.6 volts.
    b. The voltage available at the lamps will be 0.0 volts.
    c. The rheostat is working normally.
    d. More information is needed in order to determine whether the lamps will operate correctly.

18. The low speed position of the windshield wiper system shown in Figure 15 does not work; the high speed position works normally. Technician A says circuit 58 may be open. Technician B says circuit 63 may be open. Who is correct?

a. Technician A
b. Technician B
c. Both A and B
d. Neither A nor B

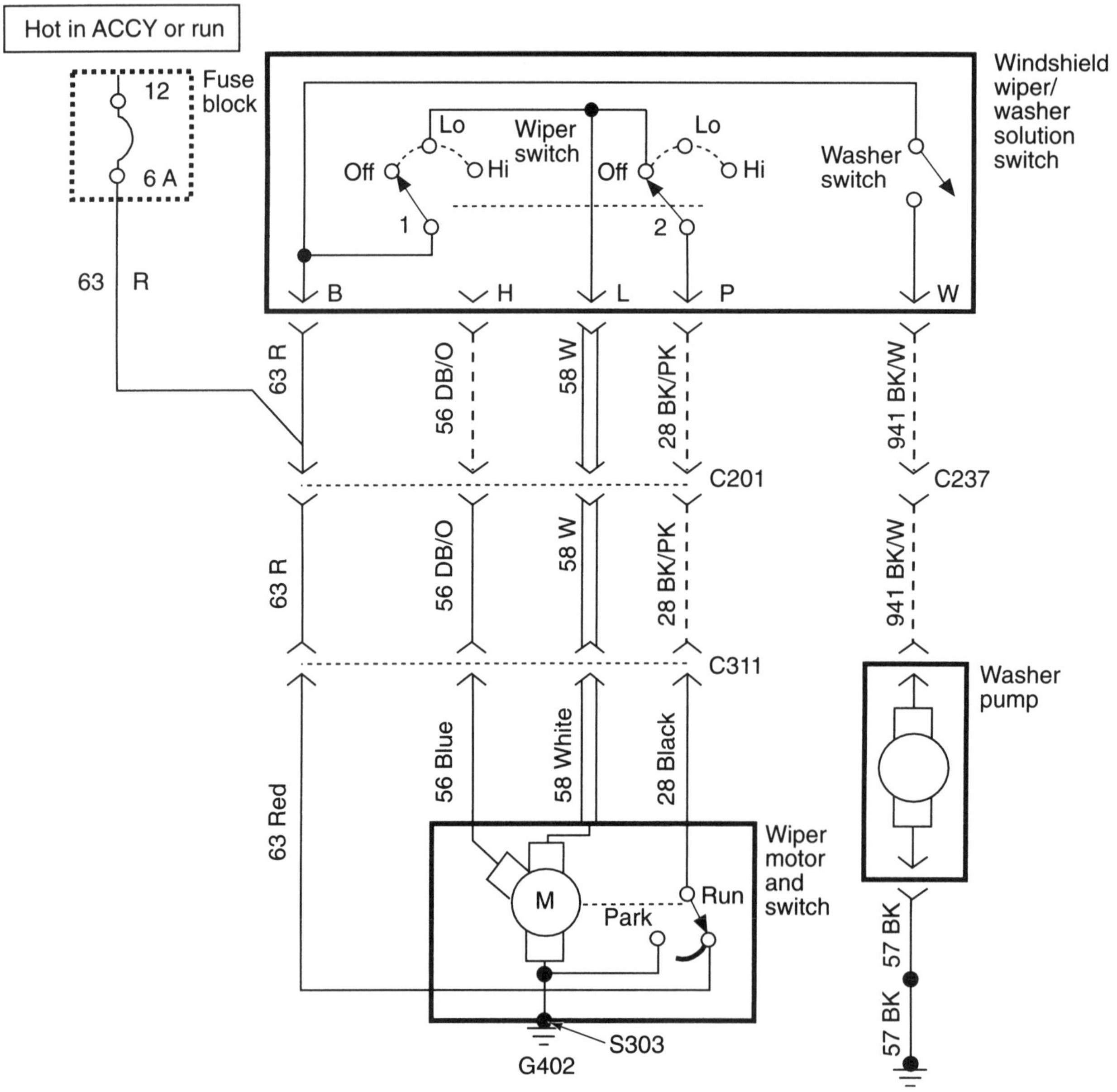

Figure 15. Two-speed wiper circuit.

19. The medium-hi speed of the blower motor circuit in Figure 16 is inoperative; the rest of the blower speeds are fine. Technician A says circuit 752 may be open. Technician B says the middle resistor in the blower motor resistor assembly may be open. Who is correct?

    a. Technician A
    b. Technician B
    c. Both A and B
    d. Neither A nor B

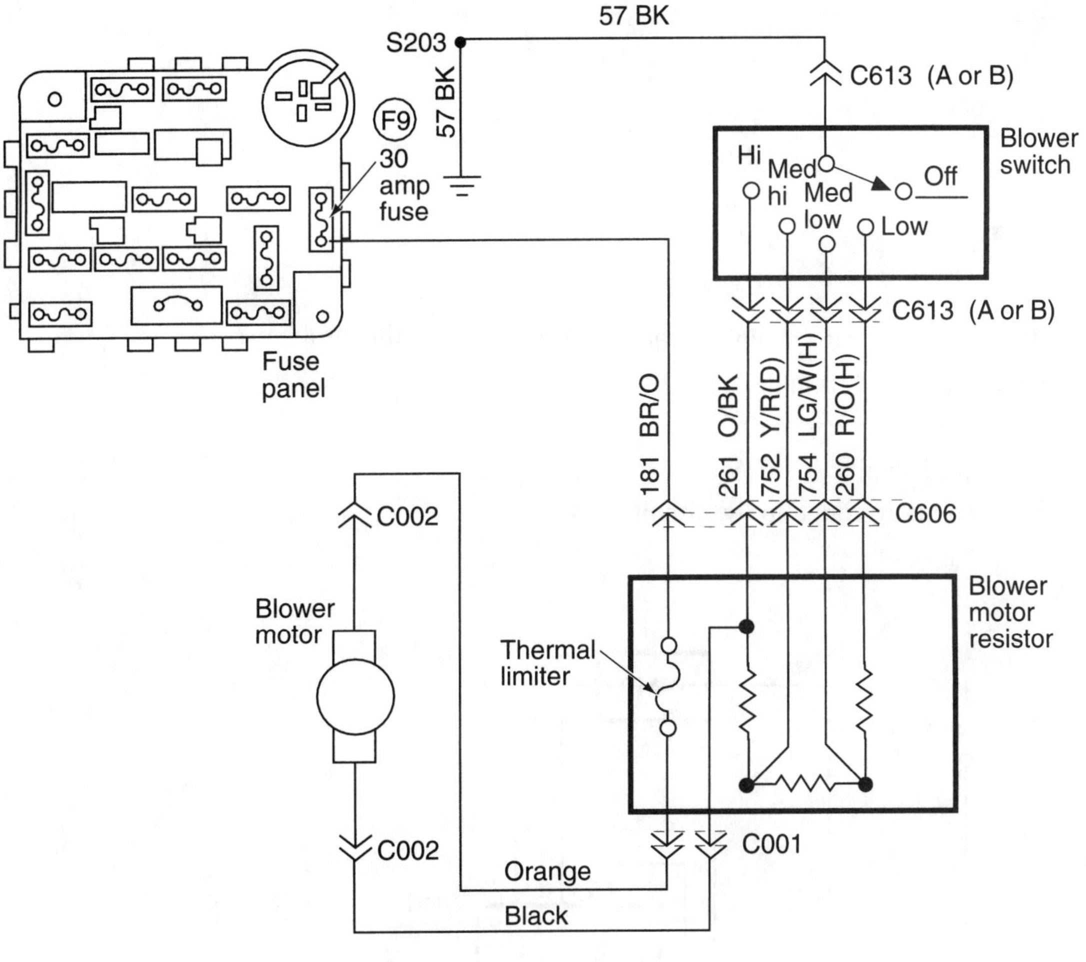

Figure 16. Blower motor circuit.

20. The power window motor in Figure 17 is completely inoperative. With the master window switch placed in the "down" position, the following voltages are measured at each terminal:

Terminal No.	Voltage
1	12V
2	0V
3	12V
4	0V
5	12V
6	12V
7	0V
8	12V
9	0V
10	12V
11	0V

Which of the following statements represents the cause of this problem?

a. The master switch is faulty.
b. The window switch is faulty.
c. The motor is faulty.
d. There is a poor ground in the circuit.

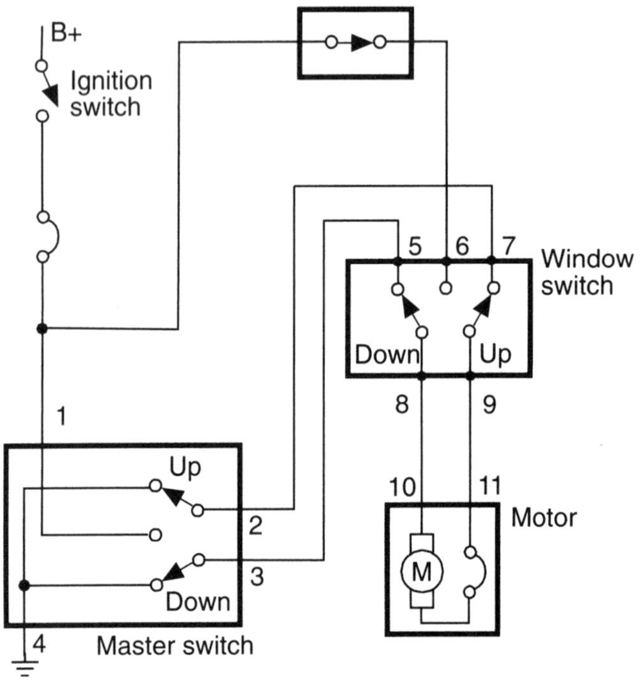

Figure 17. Power window circuit.

L'AGENT 212

BRIGADE DES EAUX

Dessin :
Daniel Kox

Scénario :
Raoul Cauvin

Couleurs : Laurent

DUPUIS

Dépôt légal : novembre 2001 — D.2001/0089/85
ISBN 2-8001-3096-2 — ISSN 0771-8004

Imprimé en Belgique.

Test à l'eau

ARTHUR TESTE UN NOUVEL ENGIN QUI, D'APRÈS LUI, NOUS ASSURERAIT PLUS DE MOBILITÉ DANS LA CIRCULATION EN CAS D'EMBOUTEILLAGE.
RAPPELLE-TOI, IL Y A QUELQUE TEMPS, IL AVAIT TESTÉ LA PLANCHE A' ROULETTES.
...OUI, JE ME SOUVIENS...
PLUS TARD, IL A ESSAYÉ LES ROLLERS...
...JE ME SOUVIENS AUSSI.
?!
AUJOURD'HUI, IL S'ATTAQUAIT A' LA TROTTINETTE...
ET ALORS ?
BEN...
430
CAUVIN - D.KOX 07

Au feu !

EH, ALBERT, QU'EST-CE QUE TU FAIS LÀ ?
LE COMMISSAIRE EST ALLÉ SE CHOISIR UN MAILLOT DE BAIN POUR LES VACANCES. IL M'A DEMANDÉ DE L'ATTENDRE ICI.
IL M'A CERTIFIÉ QU'IL N'EN AURAIT QUE POUR QUELQUES MINUTES, MAIS TU LE CONNAIS, IL EST PIRE QU'UNE GONZESSE. IL NE PARVIENT JAMAIS À SE DÉCIDER.
HMM... VOUS AVEZ FAIT VOTRE CHOIX ?
EUH... NON, À VRAI DIRE, J'HÉSITE ENTRE CES DEUX-CI !
JE PEUX LES ESSAYER ?
LA CABINE D'ESSAYAGE EST AU FOND DU MAGASIN.
MERCI.
ALLEZ, SALUT, ALBERT.
C'EST ÇA, SALUT.
HIIIIIII ! AU FEU !
RHAAA
HIIIIIIII HIIIIIII
1

ENTREE FOURNISSEURS
KOF KOF
PFF PFF
Hiiiiiiii
?
Hiiiiiii
AU SECOURS ! UN SATYRE !
?
?

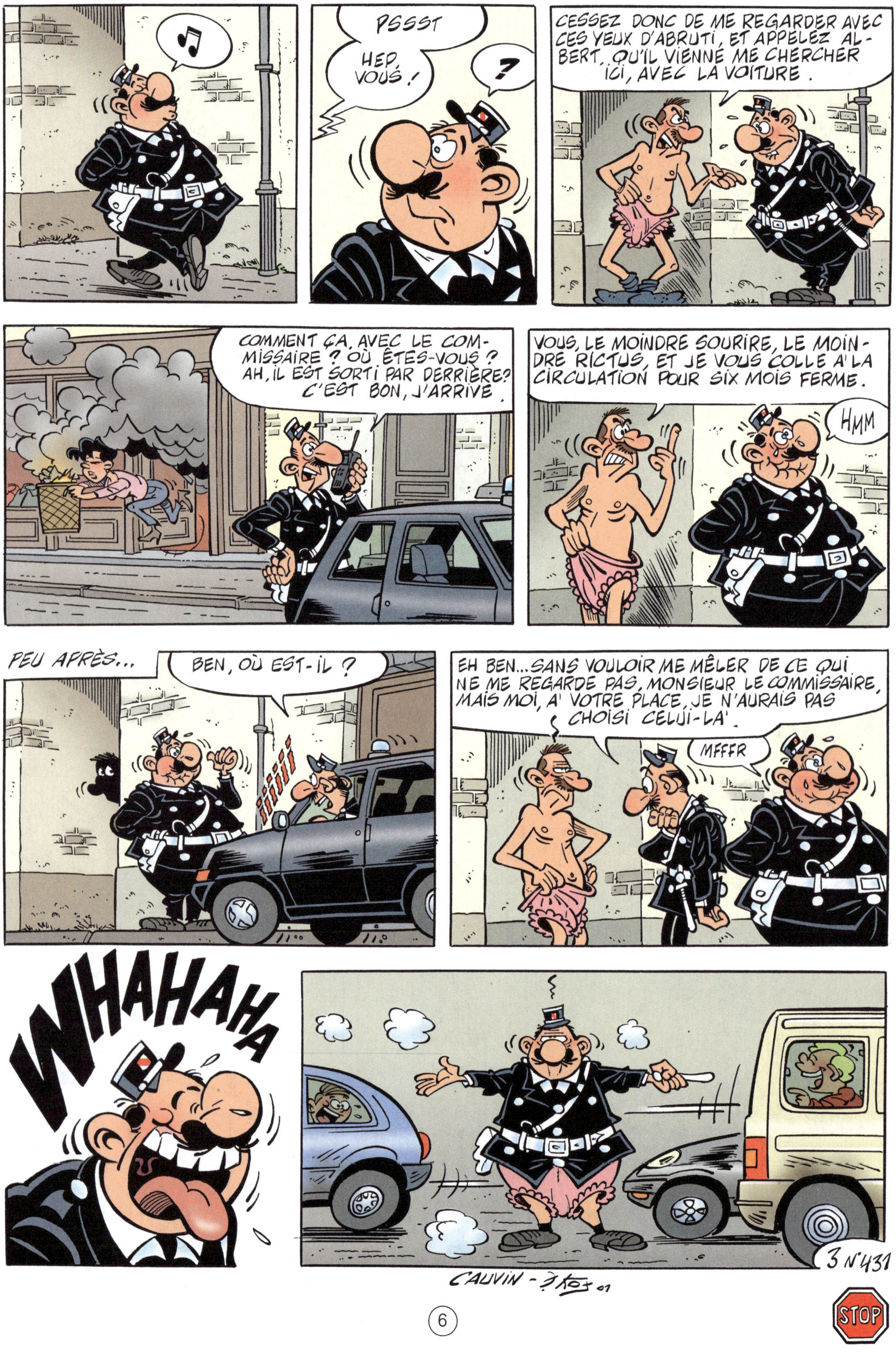
PSSST
HEP VOUS !
?
CESSEZ DONC DE ME REGARDER AVEC CES YEUX D'ABRUTI, ET APPELEZ ALBERT. QU'IL VIENNE ME CHERCHER ICI, AVEC LA VOITURE.
COMMENT ÇA, AVEC LE COMMISSAIRE ? OÙ ÊTES-VOUS ? AH, IL EST SORTI PAR DERRIÈRE? C'EST BON, J'ARRIVE.
VOUS, LE MOINDRE SOURIRE, LE MOINDRE RICTUS, ET JE VOUS COLLE À LA CIRCULATION POUR SIX MOIS FERME.
HMM
PEU APRÈS...
BEN, OÙ EST-IL ?
EH BEN...SANS VOULOIR ME MÊLER DE CE QUI NE ME REGARDE PAS, MONSIEUR LE COMMISSAIRE, MAIS MOI, À VOTRE PLACE, JE N'AURAIS PAS CHOISI CELUI-LÀ.
MFFFR
WHAHAHA
3 N°431
CAUVIN - D.KOZ 01
STOP

La loi, c'est la loi !

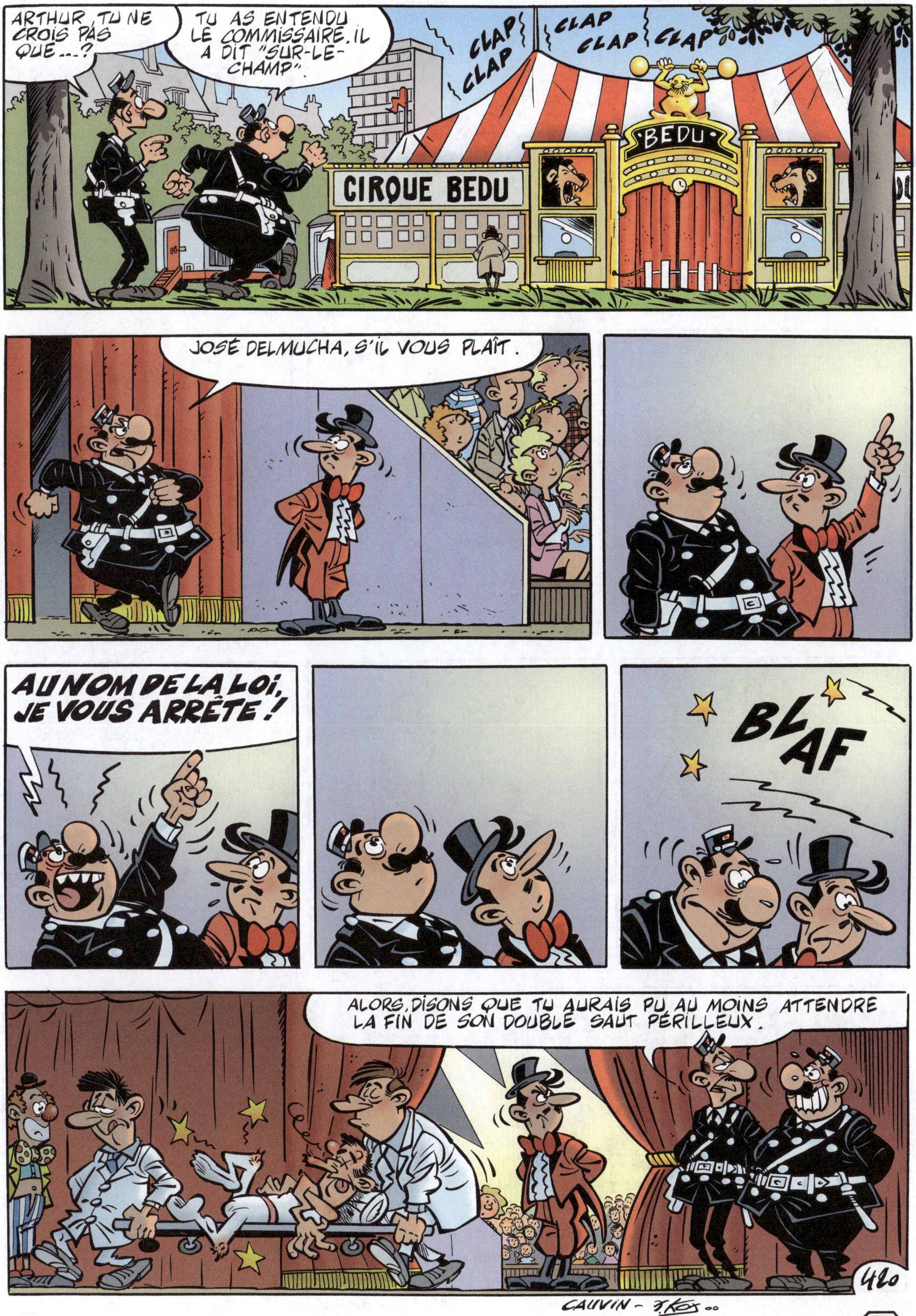

Musique à gogo

Un appel de trop !

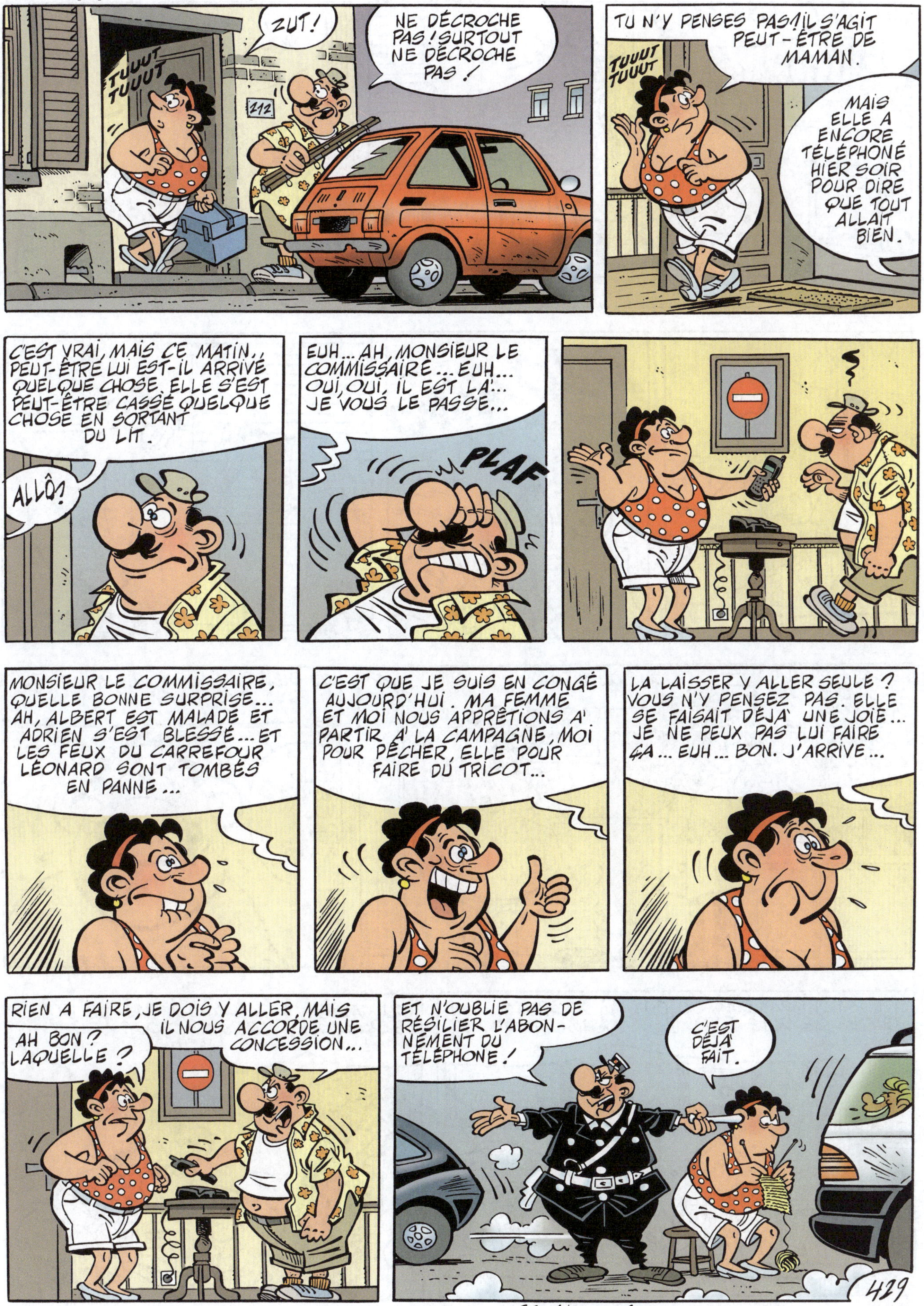

Maigrir à tout prix

ET LE LENDEMAIN...
PFF
PFF
PFF
TAGADATAGADA
?
PAF
BLAF
WAF
WAF
WAF
WAF
?
WAF
WAF
WAF
WAF
!
WAF
WAF
WAF
WAF WAF WAF
WAF WAF
2

ÇA Y EST. À MON AVIS, LES CHIENS SONT DESSUS.
WAF WAF WAF GRRR GRRR
ALLONS-Y, LES GARS. IL NE FAUDRAIT PAS RATER ÇA.
MILLE MILLIARDS, NOOON...
SULTAN, KAZAN, RAMBO, ICI !
TARA, VULCAIN, SHIRKAN, ICI !
WAF WAF WAF GRRR GRRR WAF
WAF WAF GRR GRRR
PLUS TARD...
NE VOUS INQUIÉTEZ PAS, IL S'EN SORTIRA.
A-T-IL DÉJÀ PERDU DU POIDS AU MOINS ?
OH, POUR ÇA, OUI.
IL A PERDU AU MOINS QUATRE KILOS.
DE GRAISSE ?
NOOON... UN MORCEAU DE CUISSE PAR ICI, UN MORCEAU DE MOLLET PAR LÀ...
CAUVIN
3 N°425

Chaud devant !

Halloween

!
BONSOIR, SIMPLE MORTEL. DES FRIANDISES, OU ON VOUS JETTE UN SORT.
HA HA HA, JE N'AI AUCUN BONBON SUR MOI, MAIS VOICI DE QUOI VOUS EN ACHETER.
J'ADORE L'AMBIANCE DE LA FÊTE D'HALLOWEEN.
SALUT, MORTEL DES FRIANDISES, OU JE TE JETTE UN SORT.
JE N'EN AI PAS. MAIS VOILÀ DE QUOI VOUS EN ACHETER.
OH, NOOON!
1

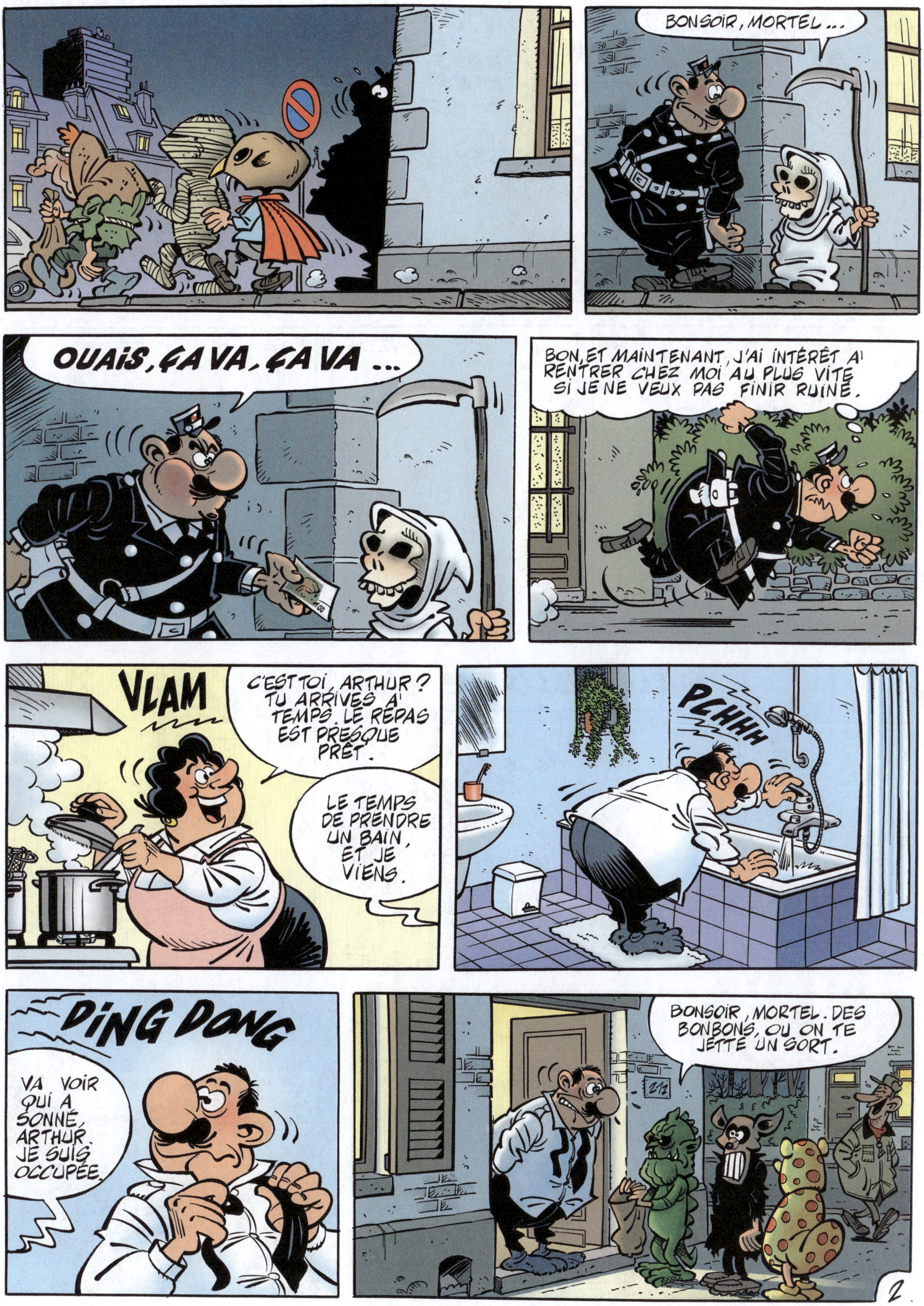
BONSOIR, MORTEL...
OUAIS, ÇA VA, ÇA VA...
BON, ET MAINTENANT, J'AI INTÉRÊT À RENTRER CHEZ MOI AU PLUS VITE SI JE NE VEUX PAS FINIR RUINÉ.
VLAM
C'EST TOI, ARTHUR ? TU ARRIVES À TEMPS. LE REPAS EST PRESQUE PRÊT.
LE TEMPS DE PRENDRE UN BAIN, ET JE VIENS.
PCHHH
DING DONG
VA VOIR QUI A SONNÉ, ARTHUR. JE SUIS OCCUPÉE.
BONSOIR, MORTEL. DES BONBONS, OU ON TE JETTE UN SORT.
2

NON MAIS C'EST PAS BIENTÔT FINI, HEIN ? DITES !
KSSS KSSS
C'EST ÇA ! C'EST ÇA ! JETEZ-MOI UN SORT. ET À PRÉSENT ALLEZ JOUER AILLEURS.
PLITCH
?
VLAM
PLITCH
MILLE MILLIARDS
PCHHH
PLITCH PLITCH
RHAAA
?
LE... LE POULET EST BRÛLÉ...
KLAK
LES PLOMBS !
3

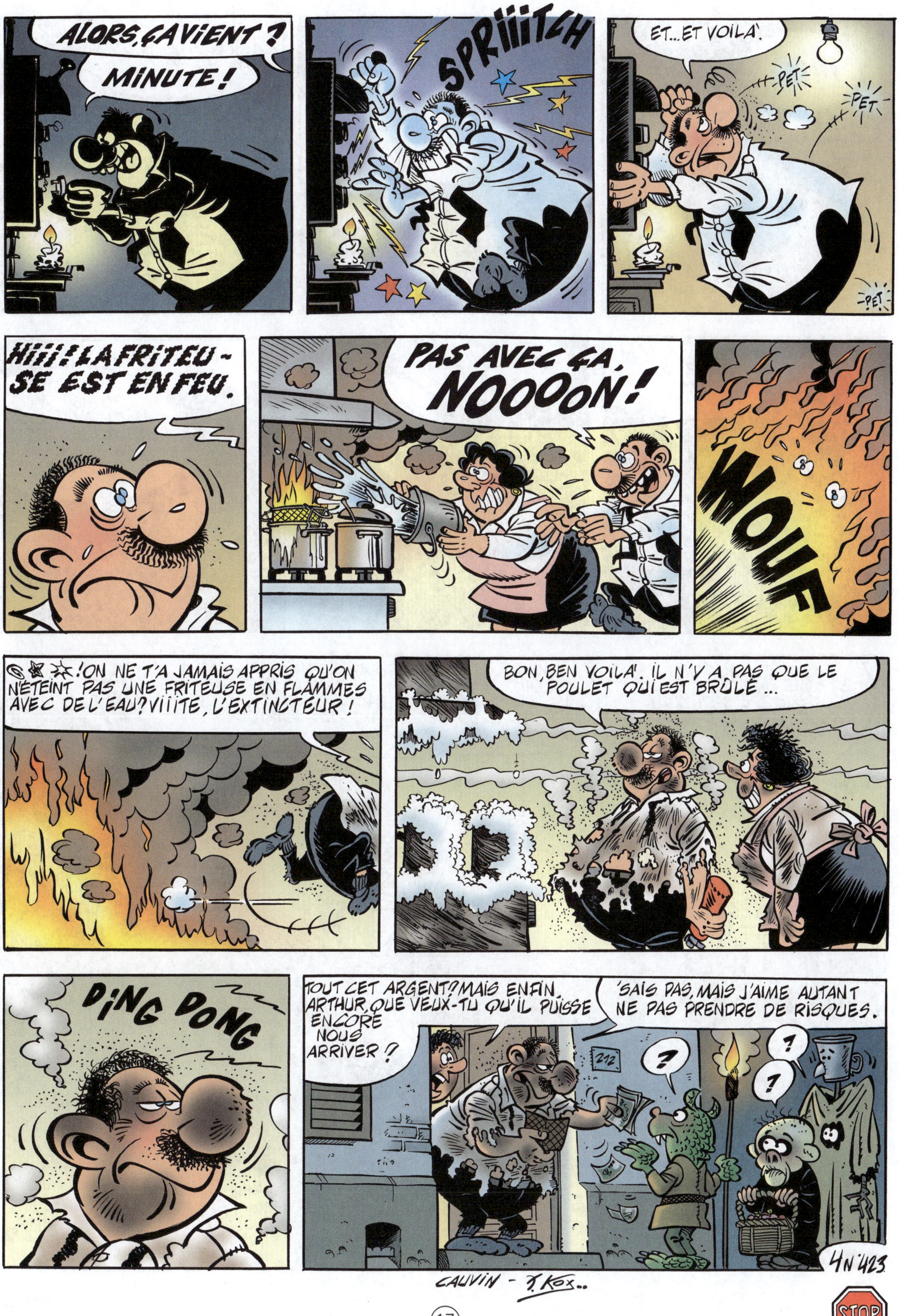
ALORS, ÇA VIENT ?
MINUTE !
SPRIIIITCH
ET... ET VOILA'.
PET
PET
PET
HIII ! LA FRITEU-SE EST EN FEU.
PAS AVEC ÇA, NOOOON !
WOUF
!ON NE T'A JAMAIS APPRIS QU'ON N'ÉTEINT PAS UNE FRITEUSE EN FLAMMES AVEC DE L'EAU? VIIITE, L'EXTINCTEUR !
BON, BEN VOILA'. IL N'Y A PAS QUE LE POULET QUI EST BRÛLÉ ...
DING DONG
TOUT CET ARGENT? MAIS ENFIN, ARTHUR, QUE VEUX-TU QU'IL PUISSE ENCORE NOUS ARRIVER ?
'SAIS PAS, MAIS J'AIME AUTANT NE PAS PRENDRE DE RISQUES.
212
?
?
?
4N'423
CAUVIN - T. KOX

Une histoire en béton

STOP

Akaï !

AKAÏ
RHAAA
BLAF
POURQUOI LE COMMISSAIRE A-T-IL FAIT APPEL A CE JAPONAIS ?
POUR NOUS APPRENDRE QUELQUES RUDIMENTS D'ARTS MARTIAUX
IL EST MINUSCULE.
LAO-TSEU A DIT "LE PETIT CHAMPIGNON PEUT AVOIR RAISON DES PLUS GRANDS CHÊNES"...
SUIVANT.
ALLEZ, ALBERT. COURAGE.
GLOPS
MAMAN...
HMM...
AKAÏ
1

RHAAAA
BLAF
SUIVANT.
?
AKAÏ
PFF
PFF
BLAF
QU'EST-CE QU'IL A VOULU DIRE PAR "LA PETITE CREVETTE GRISE NE PEUT RIEN CONTRE L'ÉLÉPHANT DE MER"?
VA SAVOIR...
?
2 N°434
CAUVIN - P. KOX 01
STOP

Grosse frayeur

VOUS VOULEZ SANS DOUTE QUE JE FASSE APPEL À LA BRIGADE SPÉCIALE D'INTERVENTION ? ALLEZ, HOP ! J'ATTENDS !
RHAAA
HOUUU
RHAAA
BOM BOM BOM
?
GRRRAT GRRRAT
2.

ACHHHH CHHHH
BONG BONG BONG BONG BONG
AGAGSCHLLLLL CHHHHHHH
ASCHHHHH
SCRATCH
ACHHHH
ACHHHH
BON SANG, MAIS QU'EST-CE QU'IL FICHE?
?
ASCHHH
ASCHHH

BON SANG, QU'EST-CE QUI VOUS PREND ?
ASCHHH AG AG
MA PAROLE, ON DIRAIT QU'IL EST DEVENU MUET.
AGA AGA
ASCHHHH
PIERRE!
AGAGA ASCHHH
AGA
QU'EST-CE QUI T'EST ARRIVÉ ?
JE TERMINAIS UNE FOS-SE QUAND TOUT S'EST ÉCROULÉ SUR MOI.
CLAC CLAC
MAIS POURQUOI NE PAS AVOIR APPELÉ ?
JE NE POUVAIS OUVRIR LA BOUCHE SANS RISQUER D'AVALER DE LA TERRE ET MOU-RIR ÉTOUFFÉ.
QUAND J'AI ENTENDU QUELQU'UN PASSER PRÈS DE MOI, TU PENSES SI JE ME SUIS ACCROCHÉ.
SANS LUI J'ÉTAIS FICHU.
OUF! TOUT EST BIEN QUI FINIT BIEN.
CLAC CLAC
MM... PAS POUR TOUT LE MONDE.
PLUS TARD...
VOUS... VOUS CROYEZ QU'IL RETROUVERA SA VOIX, DOCTEUR ?
UNE GROSSE FRAYEUR EN CHASSE UNE AUTRE. NE VOUS INQUIÉTEZ PAS, MADAME, ON S'EN OCCUPE.
ASCHHH AG
CAUVIN

Jour de carnaval

Du venin dans les veines

JE PRENAIS MON PETIT DÉJEUNER, QUAND SOUDAIN...
BOM BOM BOM
?
BOM
?
?
BLAF
A' VOTRE AVIS, QUE S'EST-IL PASSÉ ?
IL Y EN A UN QUI DOIT L'AVOIR MORDU. SOIT LE CROTALE SOIT LE NAJA. CES BESTIOLES, ÇA NE PARDONNE PAS.
ENSUITE ?
BEN, JE VOUS AI PRÉVENU...
ET UN SPÉCIALISTE EST VENU LES ENLEVER...
ZOO
TOUS CEUX QUI SONT SUR CETTE LISTE ?
OUI... ENFIN ... PRESQUE.
IL EN MANQUE UN...
HEIN ? LEQUEL?
LE BOA !

ARTHUR, OÙ EST ARTHUR ?
BEN TU LE SAIS BIEN. LE COMMISSAIRE L'A LAISSÉ DE FACTION DANS LA MAISON EN ATTENDANT LA DESCENTE DU PARQUET QUI DOIT MENER L'ENQUÊTE.
APPELLE-LE !
VIIITE !
IL... IL NE RÉPOND PAS.
TUUUT
TUUUT
POURVU QU'IL NE SOIT PAS TROP TARD !
PIUIII PIUIII
?!
CLAC CLAC CLAC
AG
LE SPÉCIALISTE ! APPELLE LE SPÉCIALISTE !
DÉSOLÉ, MAIS JE N'AI PAS PU LES SÉPARER. VENEZ LE RÉCUPÉRER AU ZOO... HA HA... C'EST BIEN LA PREMIÈRE FOIS QUE JE VOIS UN BOA AMOUREUX D'UN POULET... HAHAHA !
AG AG
3 N°422
CAUVIN - Y. KOX
STOP

Y a un truc !

ALORS LÀ, CHAPEAU ! COMMENT POUVEZ-VOUS RESTER LÀ, STOÏQUE, SOUS VOTRE UNIFORME, PAR UNE CHALEUR PAREILLE ? IL Y A UN TRUC ?
C'EST ÇA. IL Y A UN TRUC.
VROAA
TRIIIIIIT
VOUS PERMETTEZ ?
JE VOUS EN PRIE.
PAPIERS S'IL VOUS PLAÎT.
?!
418
CAUVIN - LAMBIL

Sans remède

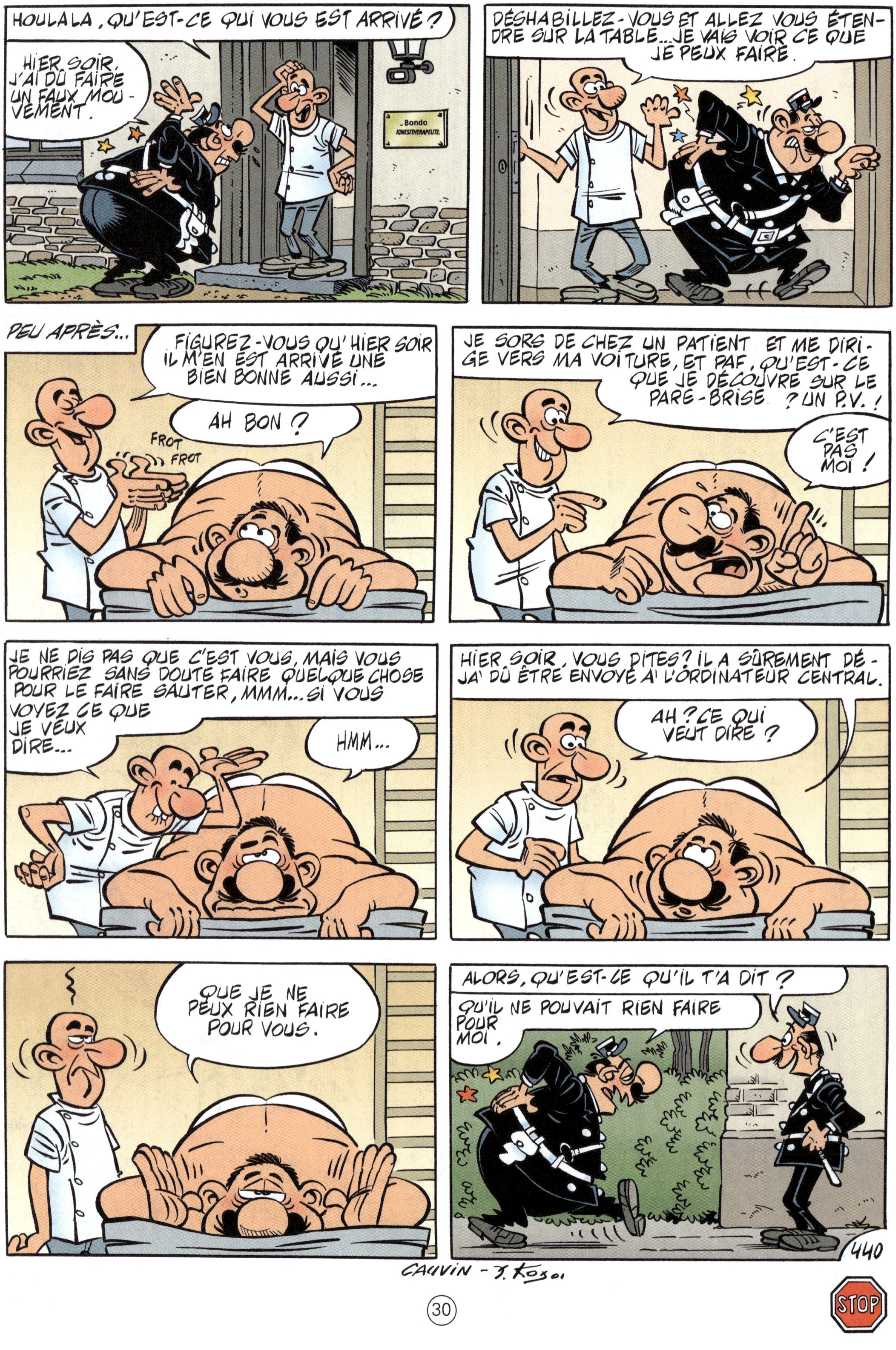
HOULALA, QU'EST-CE QUI VOUS EST ARRIVÉ ?
HIER SOIR, J'AI DÛ FAIRE UN FAUX MOUVEMENT.
Bondo KINESITHERAPEUTE
DÉSHABILLEZ-VOUS ET ALLEZ VOUS ÉTENDRE SUR LA TABLE... JE VAIS VOIR CE QUE JE PEUX FAIRE.
PEU APRÈS...
FIGUREZ-VOUS QU'HIER SOIR IL M'EN EST ARRIVÉ UNE BIEN BONNE AUSSI...
FROT FROT
AH BON ?
JE SORS DE CHEZ UN PATIENT ET ME DIRIGE VERS MA VOITURE, ET PAF, QU'EST-CE QUE JE DÉCOUVRE SUR LE PARE-BRISE ? UN P.V. !
C'EST PAS MOI !
JE NE DIS PAS QUE C'EST VOUS, MAIS VOUS POURRIEZ SANS DOUTE FAIRE QUELQUE CHOSE POUR LE FAIRE SAUTER, MMM... SI VOUS VOYEZ CE QUE JE VEUX DIRE...
HMM...
HIER SOIR, VOUS DITES ? IL A SÛREMENT DÉJÀ DÛ ÊTRE ENVOYÉ À L'ORDINATEUR CENTRAL.
AH ? CE QUI VEUT DIRE ?
QUE JE NE PEUX RIEN FAIRE POUR VOUS.
ALORS, QU'EST-CE QU'IL T'A DIT ?
QU'IL NE POUVAIT RIEN FAIRE POUR MOI.
440
CAUVIN - J. KOS 01

Baignade interdite

PLITCH
PLICH
PLICH
PLITCH
?
POK
?

DÉMARREZ, VITE !
DÉMARRE, VITE !
UNE SEMAINE QU'ILS NE S'ADRESSENT PLUS LA PAROLE ET QU'ILS S'ÉCHANGENT DES REGARDS BIZARRES, TU Y COMPRENDS QUELQUE CHOSE, TOI ?
NON. A' MON AVIS, ILS DOIVENT NOUS CACHER QUELQUE CHOSE.
3 N°436
CAUVIN - J. KOX 07

Une bonne intention

STOP

Allez jeunesse !

A' PÂQUES...
ILS LUI OFFRENT DES OEUFS...
ET QUAND L'ANNÉE SCOLAIRE EST TERMINÉE...
ILS LUI LAISSENT LIVRES ET CAHIERS...
C'EST VRAI QU'ILS ONT L'AIR FARCEURS.
ET AUJOURD'HUI, JOUR DE LA FÊTE NATIONALE, ILS NE LUI OFFRENT RIEN?
OH SI, COMME D'HABITUDE...
PAF PAF PAF PAF
PET PET PET PET
DES PÉTARDS.
CAUVIN · KOX 01
2 N°428.
STOP

Au voleur !

BIJOUTERIE
KLING KLING
VLAM
?
!
HEP, VOUS LÀ ! STOP!
?
TRIIIIT TRIIIIT
STOP, ARRÊTEZ !
AU VOLEUR!
AU VOLEUR! ARRÊTEZ-LE !
AU VOLEUR !
AU VOLEUR!
VOLEUR!
1

HÉHÉHÉ !
RHAA
IL EST COINCÉ !
ÇA Y EST, JE L'AI !
PIÉTINEZ-LE !
PENDEZ-LE !
STOOOP !
DU CALME ! DU CALME ! CET INDIVIDU A COMMIS UN DÉLIT, C'EST AU JUGE DE LE CONDAMNER, PAS À NOUS.
UN DÉLIT ? QUEL DÉLIT ? J'AI RIEN FAIT, MOI.
ET ÇA ? C'EST PAS UN DÉLIT, ÇA ? HEIN ? DITES ?
J'AI QUAND MÊME LE DROIT DE CIRCULER AVEC MA MARCHANDISE, NON ?
QUE... VOTRE... VOTRE MARCHANDISE ?
OUI, MÔSSIEUR, J'AJOUTERAI QUE JE SUIS LE PROPRIÉTAIRE DE LA BIJOUTERIE DU COIN.
M... MAIS OÙ COURIEZ-VOUS COMME ÇA ?
À L'AÉROPORT ! MAIS J'AI CHANGÉ D'AVIS, À PRÉSENT, JE VAIS COURIR AU PREMIER COMMISSARIAT VENU DÉPOSER PLAINTE CONTRE UN IMBÉCILE DE POLICIER QUI M'A FAIT RATER MON AVION !
PLUS TARD...
UNE PAROLE, C'EST UNE PAROLE ! JE RETIRERAI MA PLAINTE, À LA SEULE CONDITION QUE NOUS ARRIVIONS À TEMPS POUR LE PROCHAIN AVION.
D'AILLEURS, C'EST VOUS QUI ME L'AVEZ PROPOSÉ, NON ?
JE SAIS. JE SAIS.
STOP
2 N°435
CAUVIN - BROX 01

Au poil !

CAUVIN - J. Kox 01

Un détail

ALLÔ, TANGO A' BABA AU RHUM... TANGO A' BABA AU RHUM...
ALORS, CE BARRAGE ?
C'EST FAIT. ON A PLACÉ LES SACS DE SABLE, LA HERSE MOBILE ET LES BARBELÉS...
... NOUS AVONS MÊME MIS LE COMBI EN TRAVERS DE LA ROUTE. CROYEZ-MOI, MONSIEUR LE COMMISSAIRE, LES MALFRATS NE PASSERONT PAS.
CONTENT DE VOUS L'ENTENDRE DIRE.
OH, J'OUBLIAIS UN PETIT DÉTAIL...
JE VOUS ÉCOUTE...
BROOO
?
BROOOO
KLIKLIKLI
ET IL OSE APPELER ÇA UN DÉTAIL...
J'TE JURE !
437
GAUVIN - D. KOX 07

Date limite

?
VEUILLEZ SORTIR DE VOTRE VÉHICULE AVEC L'EXTINCTEUR, S'IL VOUS PLAÎT. C'EST UN SIMPLE CONTRÔLE.
VOUS SAVEZ VOUS EN SERVIR ?
SAIS PAS. JE N'EN AI PAS ENCORE EU L'OCCASION DE M'EN SERVIR.
SUPPOSONS QUE CE SOIT VOTRE VOITURE. ALLEZ ÉTEINDRE L'INCENDIE.
ÇA VIENT ?
HMM...
JE... JE N'AI PAS LE MODE D'EMPLOI...
HÉ HÉ
VOYEZ-VOUS ?
LE MODE D'EMPLOI EST INDIQUÉ SUR L'EXTINCTEUR.
AH ?
AH TIENS, OUI !
ALORS, C'EST POUR AUJOURD'HUI OU POUR DEMAIN ?
AVOUEZ QUE SI C'ÉTAIT RÉELLEMENT VOTRE VOITURE, ELLE AURAIT EU TOUT LE TEMPS DE CRAMER.
ATTENDEZ, J'AI PRESQUE FINI.
AH OUI... JE VOIS.
1

EH BEN C'EST PAS TROP TÔT.
CLIK
PCHHH RRRCHH PTTT PCHHH
JE M'EN DOUTAIS. LA DATE-LIMITE EST LARGEMENT DÉPASSÉE.
JE VOUS DONNE UNE SEMAINE POUR VOUS METTRE EN RÈGLE PASSÉ CE DÉLAI, CRACK, DEDANS. VU?
EUH... VU!
BON. Y EN A MARRE. CE SERA TOUT POUR AUJOURD'HUI. ON RENTRE.
A' PROPOS DE DATE-LIMITE. OÙ ON EN EST, NOUS, AVEC L'EXTINCTEUR?
ATTENDS VOIR...
CLIK
PSCHHH
EN... EN TOUS CAS, LE NÔTRE N'EST PAS PÉRIMÉ... HÉHÉ!
Z N°432
CAUVIN - F. KOS 01

D'un poulailler à l'autre...

STOP

L'imprudent

TUUUT BROOOM
PiiiP
TUUUT
POM
VRAOM TUUUT
PiiiP
BROM
EH ! OH ! OÙ COURS-TU COMME ÇA, PETIT INCONSCIENT ? TU AS ENVIE DE TE FAIRE ÉCRABOUILLER !?
BROOOM
PIP
J'VEUX MON BALLON ! J'VEUX MON BALLON !
ON VA LE RÉCUPÉRER, TON BALLON, SANS COURIR LE MOINDRE RISQUE, GRÂCE AU PRESTIGE DE L'UNIFORME.
TUT
REGARDE, JE M'APPROCHE DE LA BORDURE DU TROTTOIR, JE PRENDS MON SIFFLET, ET...
TUUUT
PiiiiP
VROM
BROOO
TRiiiiiiiT
... LA CIRCULATION S'ARRÊTE, CE QUI PERMET À MON COLLÈGUE D'ALLER RÉCUPÉRER TA BABALLE EN TOUTE SÉCURITÉ.
VA, ARTHUR.

CAUVIN - Hoz 01

Maladie de poulet

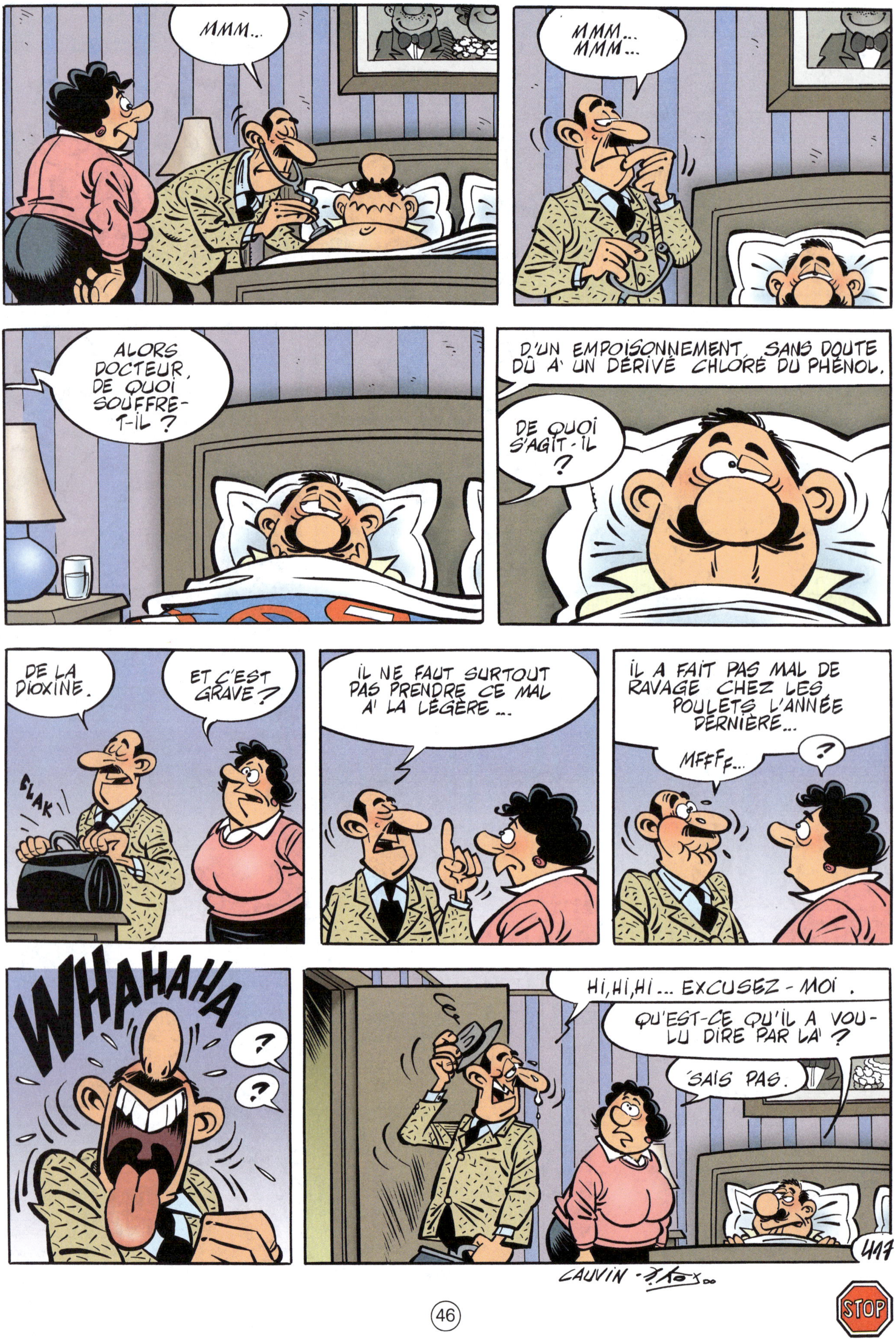